Riding
Stormy Waves

VICTORY OVER THE MARAS

Ringu Tulku Rinpoche

Edited by Maggy Jones and Mary Heneghan

Bodhicharya
PUBLICATIONS
Awaken the heart by opening the mind

First Published in 2015 by
BODHICHARYA PUBLICATIONS
Bodhicharya Publications is a Community Interest Company registered in the UK.
38 Moreland Avenue, Hereford, HR1 1BN, UK
www.bodhicharya.org   Email: publications@bodhicharya.org

©Bodhicharya Publications

Ringu Tulku asserts the moral right to be identified as the author of this work.
Please do not reproduce any part of this book without permission from the publisher.
We welcome the creation of editions of our books in other languages.
Please contact the publisher for details.

ISBN 978-1-915725-19-6
Third Edition: 2023

Edited by Maggy Jones and Mary Heneghan.

Teaching: A commentary on *'Victory over the Maras'* by Patrul Rinpoche, given at Purelands, Kagyu Samye Ling Monastery, Eskdalemuir, Langholm, Dumfriesshire, Scotland. June 2007. Transcribed and edited by Maggy Jones. Further editing by Mary Heneghan. This is also the source of most of the Short Biography of Patrul Rinpoche.

Dharma Talk: *Overcoming difficult circumstances,* Gangtok, Sikkim, India. March 2013. Transcribed and edited by Mary Heneghan. (Text on page xvii)

Bodhicharya Publications team, for this book: Annie Dibble; Margaret Ford; Mary Heneghan; Maria Hündorf-Kaiser; Maggy Jones; Mariette van Lieshout; Rachel Moffitt; Paul O'Connor; Kate Roddick; Minna Stenroos; David Tuffield & Ani Karma Wangmo.

Typesetting & Design by Paul O'Connor at Judo Design, Ireland.
Cover image: ©istockphoto.com
Inside colour image: Reproduced by kind permission from a thangka painting of Buddha and the Maras © Kagyu Samye Ling, Scotland. Photography by Peter Budd.

THE HEART WISDOM SERIES
By Ringu Tulku Rinpoche

The Ngöndro
Foundation Practices of Mahamudra

From Milk to Yoghurt
A Recipe for Living and Dying

Like Dreams and Clouds
Emptiness and Interdependence, Mahamudra and Dzogchen

Dealing with Emotions
Scattering the Clouds

Journey from Head to Heart
Along a Buddhist Path

Riding Stormy Waves
Victory over the Maras

Being Pure
The practice of Vajrasattva

Radiance of the Heart
Kindness, Compassion, Bodhicitta

Meeting Challenges
Unshaken by Life's Ups and Downs

'Obstacles are the true path
If there are no obstacles, there is no path'

Contents

Editor's Preface	xi
Buddha and the Maras	xvi
Introduction	1
The General Maras	3
Questions and Answers	12
Specific Maras: Outer and Inner	19
Questions and Answers	28
Specific Maras: Secret and Top Secret	39
Questions and Answers	49
The Causes of Maras and their Activities	59
Questions and Answers	70
The Six Remedies	79
Final Questions and Answers	97
Conclusion	111
A Short Biography of Patrul Rinpoche	123
Glossary and Notes	131
Acknowledgements	149
About the Author	151

Editor's Preface

This book is all about the maras: the obstacles and hurdles and hindrances of our life. If it ever feels more like you are navigating your way through one storm after another in your life, rather than enjoying calm waters; that is one way we could describe what it's like to be meeting the maras. So, this book is for anyone who knows that experience, would like to understand it more and seeks to learn how best to meet it.

Ringu Tulku takes us through a teaching by Patrul Rinpoche called 'Victory over the Maras.' He describes the various types of mara we may encounter; and the antidotes and qualities we can cultivate in order to overcome them. The teaching shows how maras abound at every level, from the obvious and 'external,' to the ever-more-subtle inner maras. Even the Six Paramitas, which form the basis of the Mahayana path to freedom; even these can turn into maras when we lose sight of the core intention and aspiration of the path, and start to practise them in a distorted way.

From the ultimate point of view, maras can be anything and everything that holds us back in life and prevents us from finding lasting happiness and peace, and from helping others to. They take us 'off course.' Anything that takes us away from our innate clarity, wisdom, purity and compassion can be called a mara and will lead us off course.

Maras are there whenever we are caught in delusion and confusion, whether it is gross delusion or finer and finer confusion and lack of clarity. They may seem to be external 'things' holding us back, preventing our progress and activity. But when we look closer we can see that what we are really looking at here are elements of ourselves: everything from our biggest blind spots to our subtlest tendencies, and these are so ingrained in our basic experience that we think they *are* who we are.

So, maras are all our obstacles and difficulties. But that is not the whole story. They are also all the challenges we face in life. Whether they have positive or negative outcomes rests in how we approach them. As they bring up the very things we need to overcome, we can use them to grow: they can help us become more mature, more 'grown-up.' When everything is going smoothly, and there are no maras around, we are not being given (or not noticing) a chance to develop and progress on our path. We cannot grow and mature without facing our maras.

This means maras are not something to be afraid of, or to try and avoid at all costs. We don't need to court them either; they will surely come along in life. But when they do arise we need to understand what is really happening and negotiate the situation skilfully. That is when the antidotes and remedies given in this teaching become invaluable. They give us approaches we can cultivate towards freedom from the maras, through meditation, attitude and action in the world.

The first thing is to notice when maras are arising. And then the question is how to meet them in a useful and healthy way. With an open frame of mind perhaps? A gentle heart? Kindness; compassion; and a bit of gutsy determination too? We need to grow beyond where they affect us, where they stifle our natural creativity and hold us back. To do so, we need to develop and integrate ever-deeper understanding. We need to develop wisdom. If we can really do that, we will find the maras dissolve and unravel of their own accord. They are no longer an issue and so simply dissolve, back into all that is.

This happens because all maras originate in how we see things and how we meet life. They arise from our interpretation of what is happening and the various filters we put on our perception. Maras uncover our fundamental misunderstandings and misinterpretations of reality and ourselves. So, when we finally become unhooked from a certain pattern of relating to things, we are free of that mara. It doesn't exist for us any more.

We need to remember also, that maras are not just the negative things that happen, or the things we don't like and don't want. They can just as easily seem to be terribly positive; things we like and enjoy. But anything that seduces us in such a way that it clouds our clarity and wisdom, our impartial and equanimous compassion, that is a mara. So maras include anything that attracts us to the point that we see it out of all proportion and we lose our sense of perspective. If it causes us to lose our centeredness, our direction and present-moment awareness, then we are going off course, and suffering will follow somewhere along the line.

The Buddha is traditionally said to have faced a whole range of maras. He was beset by warriors and fighting men with all manner of weapons. And he was equally seriously beset by beautiful, dancing maidens luring him away from his one-pointed quest, with promises of comfort and delight - but not freedom and not lasting happiness. He kept his seat and, gradually, through not reacting to the maras taunting, luring and attacking him, he came to a place where enlightenment dawned.

Whatever the equivalents in our own lives are, of these maras that Buddha faced and overcame; if we can encounter them and not give up our seat and not stray off course in life, then we follow in the footsteps of the Buddha. The path is to learn to stay present in our heart with honesty, clarity, wisdom and compassion, throughout the ups and downs. This is the path of freedom and release from suffering. So, what better course to steer?

Although Patrul Rinpoche originally gave his teaching in the 19th Century, the wisdom he shared is timeless. You will hopefully find it is completely relevant to our modern lives and provides a helpful framework to engage with them. Ringu Tulku takes us through each point of Patrul Rinpoche's teaching, translating and explaining it; so that we can relate

Editor's Preface   xiii

this understanding to the problems we ourselves encounter. Overall, these teachings can provide the clarity to cut through our fetters, and our excuses, and help us steer a truer course through life. We hope you enjoy the book and find chances to bring these teachings onto the path of your life. May they help you face whatever hurdles and hindrances you come across.

Ringu Tulku gave the teachings that form this book at a small retreat held at Purelands Retreat Centre, Kagyu Samye Ling, Scotland, in the summer of 2007. We are indebted to Samye Ling for organizing this and allowing Bodhicharya Publications to publish these teachings in this way. May they bring true freedom from suffering. May this spread far and wide, so that ultimately all beings may find their way through the stormy waves, to complete liberation.

Mary Heneghan
For Bodhicharya Publications
Sikkim, March 2014

xv

'*Buddha and the Maras*' - section from thangka painting © Kagyu Samye Ling

xviii

'Obstacles are the true path.
If there are no obstacles, there is no path.'

This is how it is usually said to be and I think this has a deep meaning.
The path is something by which you change your usual way of reacting;
you overcome your usual way of being and your habitual tendencies; you
transform them. If everything goes as usual, you cannot transform. There
is no need to. There is no challenge or necessity to change.
There is no compulsion to change and nothing instigates change.

But if there is an obstacle, then there is a challenge. You have to react to
it, either in a bad way or in a good way. If you react to that challenge in
a good way, that is the practice. You need something, that you then have
the choice of how to react to it, how to negotiate it, in order to proceed on
the path. If there is no obstacle to negotiate, then there is no path. So,
therefore, if there are obstructions or obstacles,
they are regarded as a very good thing!

If someone can take obstructions as their path, then they are a good
Dharma practitioner. How strong a Dharma practitioner you are can be
seen by how well you can take any obstruction as your path.
Whether you can really overcome the obstacles or hindrances
that come your way, depends on this.

Whether you become enlightened, or not, depends on whether you can
successfully cross the maras.

xx

Introduction

According to Patrul Rinpoche, one should not give teachings on something that does not give benefit to beings, even if it is something you understand well. So maybe we should ask, right at the start:

Is this a topic you would like to hear about ... ?

The teaching we are going to look at here is one that Patrul Rinpoche took from a variety of sources within the Sutras taught by Buddha. He then wrote this teaching to bring all the essential points together in one text. He says the text is 'To examine the causes of the maras, and how to get rid of them; how to abandon them.' The name of the book is an instruction in itself: *Victory Over the Maras*. The text describes how we can achieve this.

'Mara' can be translated as 'demons' or 'obstructions' or 'obscurations' – something that becomes a hurdle or a hindrance. Sometimes maras may be described as beings coming to tempt one, like in the story of Buddha before he became enlightened. First, the maras came in the form of very beautiful women, who danced around Buddha, saying, 'What you are doing is pointless... Come with us, and enjoy yourself... All this meditation will get you nowhere...' They tried to seduce him.

When that didn't work, more maras came in the form of a furious and terrifying army of devils, who threw weapons and fire and a rain of thunderbolts at him, saying, 'If you don't leave this place, we will kill you and all your family.' But none of these things – neither desire, nor fear - could waver him; and thus he became enlightened. Those maras, in a way, were both symbolic and experiential.

This text starts with a traditional homage and a promise to write, which is how Tibetan texts usually begin:

May all beings win victory over the maras.

To the Refuge of all beings, the ones who are the Buddha, Dharma and Sangha, and, inseparable from the Buddha and his heirs, the Bodhisattvas: I bow down; I make supplications; I pay homage.

For the benefit of beings, the Buddha taught these instructions on how to examine the maras, and these pith instructions I have collected here and written down.

Generally, for someone who is on the path, unless they have attained enlightenment or complete realisation, there are always certain obstacles and different kinds of misconceptions, obscurations or maras. But you can say there are two *main* types of maras: general maras and particular maras. We shall first discuss the general maras.

The General Maras

1. The Mara of Kleshas

The first of these general maras is the mara of klesha. *Klesha* is a Sanskrit word. It is sometimes translated as 'mind poison' or 'afflictive emotion' and it covers all distressing, or negative, emotions and states of mind. The three main kleshas are: aversion, attachment and ignorance; ignorance meaning a state of mind of confusion or not knowing yourself and not knowing the nature of things.

These three are called the three root mind poisons. In addition to these, we have jealousy and pride, which are a combination of these root poisons. Jealousy is regarded as a combination of aversion and attachment; and pride is a combination of ignorance and attachment. There are many possible combinations and divisions and together they make up a myriad of afflictive emotions or kleshas.

This mara of afflictive emotions is the main obstacle to the happiness of beings. It brings unhappiness and suffering to ourselves; and creates problems and does harm to others as well. It is the main hurdle to finding lasting peace and happiness.

2. The Mara of Aggregates

'The mara of aggregates' is the name of this mara, and it refers to our self-clinging to the five aggregates [or 'bundles'] that make up our being. We cling to our experience of ourselves; to this continuum; to our body, our mind and our feelings. We make an identity. We assert 'This is **me**' and then we cling to it. And because of this, our whole way of reacting to everything that happens is affected. 'I' become the centre of the world; everything else is either *for* me or *against* me, and because of this all my reactions are coloured with either aversion or attachment and the other kleshas.

3. The Mara of the Lord of Death

This is impermanence. Things change. We die, life finishes. There is no certainty except that everybody dies and everything changes. Death does not always come according to age; there is nothing certain. It is not that you grow old and then you die. You may be young but there is no certainty that you are not going to die. You are healthy now, but there is no certainty that you are not going to die. You can be intelligent, or successful, or beautiful – or whatever – the timing of the Lord of Death is uncertain. It is a mara, because if you are on the path trying to attain enlightenment or working in some way on yourself, and then suddenly you die, that is a problem!

4. The Mara of Devas

The fourth of the general maras is the mara of Devas, or the mara of the 'god realm'. This is when everything is good; everything is nice. Sometimes is it is called the 'Child of the Gods' or the 'Heavenly Mara'. It refers to when everything is good and everything you do is successful, so you become self-important, complacent, self-satisfied and think you are 'the greatest'. It is about pride.

Arrogance is perhaps a more appropriate term here, arrogance that is not simply being arrogant but includes also self-importance and a kind of delusion of grandeur. Arrogance is regarded as something very bad from this point of view, because an arrogant person thinks they have nothing more to learn, so they cannot improve any more. They are like a stone, which has been polished with plenty of oil so that, no matter how much water you pour over it, the water just runs away and the stone stays dry and shiny.

These are the four general maras. We all have these maras. We are all under the power of these four maras. And it is because we are under the power of these four maras that we are not enlightened, that we do not achieve full realisation. Because of these maras, we have problems and suffering and remain in a samsaric state of being. That is how it is understood.

There are four sub-sections of the mara of Devas:

4.1 The Mara of Conflict is the first sub-section of the mara of devas. It causes fighting, makes you argue with people and have disagreements, things like that. If you say things that are hurtful, we could say that this mara is influencing you.

4.2 The Mara of Distraction brings the desire to accumulate or gather together things that will distract your mind. All sorts of things. Sometimes your mind says, 'I want this! I need this... I really must have this and this...' many sorts of things. But you do not - you really do not - need them at all.

Alternatively, sometimes you might feel sleepy or lazy or kind of dull, so you don't want to do positive things, like study, reflection and meditation. You are taken away from doing anything that is useful or positive or necessary. This mara is not actually harmful but you do nothing useful and this is the mara of distraction.

4.3 The Mara of Great Desire is developing too much desire and too much need to have possessions, or experiences. You say, 'I want this; I must have that!' Even if you have more than you need, you cannot give anything away because you think you don't have enough. 'I need it for the future; I need it for my children; I need it for my grandchildren; I

The General Maras 5

need it for...' all sorts of things. Even if you don't have anywhere to put all your things, you still want more. Even if you have no place left to walk through, or to sit, you still pile things up.

I hope there is nobody like that here? My uncle says I am a bit like that with regard to books. My table is always full, my bed is full; in fact my whole bedroom is full. Then, when I am away, he goes in and throws everything out. I have written countless articles about all sorts of things – all thrown out! Anyway, it doesn't matter, that is very good.

Whereas this enormously strong attachment, the mara of great desire, means that even if you give a little thing to somebody, you feel as though it is being cut from your flesh. You can still remain completely attached to things, even when you give them away.

4.4 The Mara of Turning Your Mind away from your Path. This mara is more likely to come to Dharma practitioners, including monks and nuns. You want to work on something, and then immediately something comes up, 'Oh if I do this I shall miss this, then I wouldn't be able to do this, then I could not do this...' and things like that. Something comes up in your mind that turns it away from doing something positive.

Even if you are committed to your path, there can be too many other things coming up in your mind. You cannot take your mind off those things and they turn you away from your path, from a positive approach. You have dreams of doing certain things, thinking again and again 'I shouldn't do this but I want to do this'. Things like that, so your mind turns towards something that you truly know is not the right thing to do, but your mind always turns towards that.

The text says that maras can come in the form of things, in the form of beings, in the form of thoughts and emotions and in the form of incidents. And, in whatever form they come, they will obstruct you from doing anything positive and turn you away from your path.

It is also said that there are many negative kinds of spirits and beings, who are able to, and who want to, obstruct people. These obstructions and maras can manifest in many different ways. They can appear as something very negative or bad, like in the form of illnesses or death; or in the form of unfavourable things such as the demons that appeared to the Buddha before enlightenment.

Maras can also appear in the form of seemingly very attractive things, positive things, which can bring strong attachment. Fear and clinging – when these two kleshas become too strong, then they become maras; they become an obstacle.

The story of the two spirits

We have so many spirits in Tibetan Buddhism! There are eight main classes of spirits, which can be further sub-divided into hundreds. You could research these spirits your whole life. I don't know whether you can see them or not, but descriptions of them are given.

In this story, there are two spirits: one is a *gyalpo* and the other is a *tsen*. A tsen is usually red in colour and sometimes rides a red horse. He is very swift, and very quick to strike. The gyalpo is much more subtle. Gyalpos are usually – maybe I shouldn't say this – Lamas who turn bad!

So, one day a gyalpo and a tsen happened to meet on the road. They greeted each other and the tsen said, 'How much harm can you do to other beings?' And the gyalpo said, 'Well, I can do much better than you!' and the tsen said, 'No! I can do more harm than you!' So they agreed to have a contest to see who could inflict the most harm.

They looked around; the place was deserted. Then they saw two Lamas sitting in caves nearby and they said, 'Let us take those two Lamas sitting in those caves practising Dharma. We can have one each and we shall see who can do the most harm.'

They chose one Lama each and the tsen went up and immediately pushed one of the Lamas over the cliff. The Lama fell to the bottom and died. The tsen came back and said, 'Look what I've done! What are you

The General Maras   7

going to do? You are just sitting here!' The gyalpo laughed and said, 'You think you have harmed him? You are thick! Look at him!' So they looked, and this Lama's consciousness had gone straight up to Dewachen. 'You just liberated him!' said the gyalpo. 'You call that harming someone? You are useless! Now, just watch me and see how I deal with this other Lama'.

At first, everything went well for the other Lama. Whenever he gave a blessing to somebody, that person became well. Even the rice he threw outside his cave, grew and sprouted and flourished. Everybody was a bit surprised as it was so impressive. Everything he did became so successful, and brought so much benefit. He could even perform miracles.

The Lama became more and more famous, more and more successful and richer and richer. After a while, he moved out of his cave to the town where he found the most beautiful girl and married her. By then he has activities everywhere. He has become so successful, so rich, and so powerful that many people surround him. He has too many friends, and too many enemies. Conflicts arise, leading to skirmishes, debates, court cases and fighting. Until, one night, his enemies come and attack him and kill him.

By the time this Lama dies, however, he has completely lost all his Dharma practice. He is fully engrossed in the samsaric approach. His consciousness becomes the slave of the gyalpo who turns to the tsen, and says, 'This is how I do it!'

So obstacles sometimes come in the form of success, in the form of seemingly good things. Sometimes, even when you see something like a vision of the Buddha, it may not necessarily be a true vision of the Buddha. It could be a mara causing you to react something like: 'Oh I have had a vision of Buddha. I must be a very special person!' So you develop pride and all the things that follow, and the vision is not beneficial. Whatever makes you arrogant, self-important and causes you to lose your Bodhicitta, so that you become self-centred or anything like that, is a mara.

It is usually said that if you have a vision of a Buddha or a Bodhisattva, or something similar, you can tell whether it is a positive or a negative vision by two things. Firstly, by what kind of feeling you have from it. Secondly, by what kind of smell is present. It is said that if a vision comes and you feel a bit uneasy, or irritated – not really happy – even if you see a Buddha, it is not correct; it is a mara, an obstacle. But if, when you have a vision, even if it looks like a demon, or something really negative, if you have peace of mind and you feel joyful or relaxed, then it is positive. Then sometimes there is a smell present with a vision. If there is a filthy smell like rotten garlic, then it is not positive. But if there is a really sweet fragrant smell, like a flower or like sandalwood, that is a sign that it is a true vision. The smell is the surest sign.

The purpose of maras

The text asks why there are obstacles and maras. Why do obstacles and maras come? And why do they especially come to those who are trying to do something positive, to liberate themselves, to work on themselves and to keep to the path? The example that is given is to imagine that you are under the power of somebody; you are the slave of somebody. And you are trying to get out of that position; you revolt against your slavery. You are on the way to freedom; you are escaping. The one who is in charge of you, who has power over you, will try to prevent that. In a similar way, when we are working to free ourselves from a samsaric state of mind and samsaric way of being, with its delusion and confusion, then the maras who have been controlling us try to prevent us from becoming free.

The more positive you become, the more likely it is that there will be obstacles. The obstacles become stronger and sharper. Therefore, we should not expect that if we are doing something good, there will not be any obstacles. This is a key thing to understand. This is not the way to think. The way to think is: The more I do positive things and the more I advance in a positive way, the more the maras will come. The maras' activity will increase and the obstacles I face will become stronger and clearer. Just like if I was in a prison, if I am to escape I have to cross those walls, those barriers. The further I want to go from the prison, the more barriers I will have to cross and the stronger they will be. That is the understanding.

It is very important to realise this, and be able to face this, and cross over the hurdles. We must not think there will be no problems, that it will all be smooth because, if we think like that, we will collapse like a flat tyre at the first hurdle!

Student: Is there a comparison with a mountain: the higher up you go, the steeper it becomes?

Rinpoche: Yes, that's right. Exactly the same way. There is always a fight between good and evil, it is a little bit like that. The more you emerge from an imprisoned state, an overpowered state, toward a state of freedom; the more obstacles will confront you. But it has to be understood that there will also be more support, more help, more blessings and more encouragement. It is said that if somebody is really genuinely practising Dharma, the extent of their commitment and diligence actually affects the strength of obstacles. It is like that.

There is a well-known quotation from the Sutra called 'The Display of Manjushri Sutra': One heavenly person asks Manjushri, 'Where do the maras of the Bodhisattvas come from?'

Manjushri replies, 'Lhay-bu [Son of the Gods], the maras of the Bodhisattvas come from their diligence in their practice of the Dharma'.

When he is asked why that is, Manjushri explains that if you are not diligent, if you are not genuinely and industriously practising Dharma, there won't be any additional mara obstacles - because *that is* the mara! Laziness is a mara. So, if you are following the mara of laziness, there won't be any resistance from mara. You are going with it so there is no resistance. The more you resist the mara, the stronger the mara activity, or obstacles will become.

Patrul Rinpoche says here that when you do nothing at all, or when you are totally under the control of the maras or in their power, then you experience no obstacles and no resistance from the maras. When you try to get out of that situation, however, then there will be obstacles and resistance from maras. The stronger you try, the stronger the resistance.

Overcoming the maras

Whether you will be able to overcome the resistance of the maras depends on many things. Merit is one support. The amount of merit you have accumulated, in this life and earlier lives will help. Whether you have been under the guidance of a good 'spiritual friend' or not, that also makes a difference. Whether you are intelligent and your faculties are clear or not, that makes a difference. Other things that make a difference are: How strong your courage is; whether you have strong, clear instructions and know how to work on them or not; and whether your mind is very stable and determined, or not. Whether the maras will stop you, or whether you can overcome them, will depend on all these things.

Maras' obstacles will always be there so it is important to examine and clearly understand the maras and try to work on them. The ways and methods to counteract these four general maras - the remedies to these maras - will be discussed later in the text.

The General Maras 11

Questions and Answers

Help from Buddhas and Bodhisattvas

Student: Can you tell us about Guru Rinpoche and his role in helping us overcome the maras?

Rinpoche: It is important to understand that mara is anything that is an obstacle. Mara can be the kleshas - your very own mind poisons. Ultimately, it is all about your own experience. Obstruction can seemingly come from something outside, but whether that outside thing is an obstacle or not depends on you and how you experience it. So therefore, in this way, maras ultimately all come from within. This is just one way of looking at it, though, one viewpoint. We are in a samsaric state of mind and are not free. We are under the power of our mind poisons; we are under the power of our own wrong view and ignorance. We are under the power of our habitual tendencies and our own karmic conditions. We are under the power of many such influences and thus are not free. And all these things are maras.

These things that we call maras are obstructing us from being free from suffering and ignorance. They stop us enjoying lasting peace and happiness. The practice of Dharma is about finding this freedom from suffering and ignorance; finding liberation and lasting peace and happiness. Our efforts are all towards that. But when we make steps towards freedom, there are still these strong things that prevent us being free. So these are then experienced as obstacles, which can prevent us progressing further toward that freedom.

The aim of Buddhas and Bodhisattvas is to help people to be free, to prevent them from being stopped by these obstacles. That's what we call 'helping people', isn't it? Receiving blessings gives support and helps people to be free. Receiving teachings and instructions also helps people to find their way out of samsara. Receiving positive guidance and healing is all about freeing people. So all the activities of the Buddhas and Bodhisattvas are towards that end; all their efforts are to clear the maras and the hurdles from our path.

The problem is we cannot receive the blessings or teachings direct from the Buddhas and Bodhisattvas, because of being under the sway of the maras. Because of the maras, we cannot open ourselves directly to the blessings available. Instead we struggle. The Buddha Shakyamuni and Bodhisattvas like Guru Padmasambhava and Chenrezig, all dedicated their wisdom and the accumulation of all their positive deeds, eon after eon, lifetime after lifetime, to helping beings find happiness. They dedicated their positive deeds so that they might grow strong, so that when times are very difficult and peoples' minds are strongly negative and in conflict, greedy and aggressive; their power could become even stronger in order to be able to help in such difficult times. And this was a dedication of Guru Padmasambhava (or Guru Rinpoche) in particular.

Guru Rinpoche left guidance in teachings that he buried for such times. This is a rather strange Tibetan practice - what we call *terma* or 'treasure findings'. It is said that Guru Rinpoche saw the future of Tibet and the world, and then prophesied that at a certain time, when certain things would happen, particular practices and teachings would become very powerful and beneficial.

He asked his disciple, Yeshe Tsogyal, to write these teachings down and through some special miraculous power it happened that a particular teacher or person would discover the teaching at the correct time – not before, not after, but only at the specific, correct time. This person who finds the teaching is called a *terton* or 'treasure finder' and they would generally be some kind of blessed person or emanation of Guru Rinpoche or would have some connection with him. Guru Rinpoche said that when the terma is discovered, and that teaching is practised, it would have a special influence on that time.

The General Maras   13

There are many examples like this, which is why Guru Rinpoche is said to be especially powerful. And maybe it is true with every Bodhisattva. The stronger and worse the Dark Age becomes, the stronger the negative emotions of the people become; the stronger the power of the Bodhisattvas will become. It could be that it happens like that. It could be that if you think it is like that, then it becomes like that. Sometimes, it is a matter of confidence. If you really have confidence in something, then it happens like that. This could be a part of the truth. So if you think Guru Rinpoche said he would be strong right now, and have real confidence in that, then he must be strong right now!

The higher you go, the steeper it becomes

Student: How is it that even highly realised Lamas can sometimes behave very badly?

Rinpoche: Well - I don't think it is always like this - but one thing that is said is: 'The higher you go, the steeper it becomes'. This means that the 'higher' you are, the harder the obstacles. The maras and their activity will become stronger than when you are a 'lesser' person 'down there'. But of course a 'high' Lama is not necessarily the most 'realised' Lama. 'High' can just mean their rank. It can be just because they have a big monastery. The head of a large monastery would be considered a high Lama but would not necessarily be highly realised.

There is a story about a Lama from some time ago who was a high Lama and the head of a big monastery. One day a Tibetan, just an ordinary Khampa [a person from the district of Kham in Tibet], came to see him and said, 'I have a question for you. There is something I don't understand.'

The Lama said, 'What is that?'

'I don't understand this tulku system. When we look at history and hear the stories, the first Lama at the beginning is very highly realised.

He is a great scholar, he has great realisation and great compassion; he is a very great Master. He has not very many followers, his monastery is not very big, he is not rich; he is poor but he is greatly realised. Then he sets up his monastery. When his next incarnation comes, his monastery is much bigger, the followers are more numerous and his labrang [private household or Trust, see later] is much richer.

But the Lama himself is not as great! He is less learned, less realised and doesn't seem that compassionate. Then when the third reincarnation comes, it is even more so! The monastery is even bigger, richer and more elaborate and there are even more monks. But the Lama has not grown in realisation, he has even less realisation. All these things I see, but why is it so? I don't understand because the Lama should become more and more realised and more and more superior, but it does not turn out like that!'

The Lama just listened to his question and said nothing. Then after two or three days, he disappeared. Everyone was very worried, 'What has happened to our Lama? He has just vanished!' And they searched everywhere for him. Then finally, after many months, they found him in a very remote corner of the district, sitting in a cave. They all crowded round and said, 'What is wrong? Did anything go wrong? Did someone say something bad or against you? Why are you running away like this? You are an important Lama. You are our main guide, our guru!'

'No, nobody did anything to me' he replied, 'but I was asked this question and I realised why things are like that. The first Lama? He studied, he practised, he did retreats, and he became a highly realised person. In his next birth, this Lama had more things to do for his monastery, for all his people, so he did less study, and less practice. And the third reincarnation did even less. So if I stay in the monastery I shall do less practice. But I want to practice.' So he didn't want to return to the people and the monastery.

This is one story. It is also possible that a Lama who is a high Lama may not necessarily be highly realised. Another possibility is that a great

The General Maras   15

master or a great Bodhisattva may do things that are seemingly negative but in the long run they may be very good and very beneficial. Some apparently strange Lama activities can be of that kind also.

There is a story of Gesar of Ling. Gesar of Ling is a Tibetan epic and is said to be the longest epic in the world! The longest version on record is two hundred volumes. It has some very strange characters in it. In one story, Gesar is a Bodhisattva who comes down to help beings fight against the negative forces. Many great Bodhisattvas come to assist him as his captains and ministers. One of these is his uncle and an emanation of Hayagriva, a very great being like a Buddha. In the human world, this uncle does everything possible to put obstacles in Gesar's way. He tries to kill him, tries to deceive him and does every destructive and harmful thing he can think of to stop Gesar.

But everything negative that the uncle does to stop Gesar, or to harm him, becomes positive in the end because many other problems are solved on the way. So his seemingly hostile activities become a kind of catalyst to produce victory. Finally the uncle's activity (even though it was not done with good intentions) actually becomes something very helpful and things turn out better because the uncle was there doing these things. We can never know exactly how things will turn out.

Usually when there are problems in the Kagyu lineage or similar, the problem doesn't have anything to do with Dharma. The problem itself is usually more an administrative or organisational problem. Problems can also arise here due to the differences between old and new systems.

For instance, in Tibet, each Lama has a *labrang*, which is like the Trust of the Lama. All the income of the Lama goes to this labrang and it is managed by the people who are looking after the Lama: the family or monks or a group of people. All the expenditure on behalf of the Lama is met by this Trust. When the Lama dies they do all the things that are needed for his or her cremation, and then keep this labrang going for the next incarnation. They are responsible for recognising the next incarnation and organising their enthronement and education and everything. Then when he or she is old enough, any income from their work goes to the labrang again.

In the modern world, in the West and in India, a labrang is not legally recognised, so a Trust has to be set up, or a committee or something like that. Then the problem of who is in charge arises: the labrang or the Trust? And there can be a clash. The issue can even go to court. But it is basically a clash between different systems and different understanding. There can be a lot of confusion; many Lamas, even high Lamas, don't really know what a 'Trust' is. So there can be misunderstandings and conflicts within Dharma circles, and involving Lamas, which are not based on Dharma but on practicalities.

18

Specific Maras: Outer and Inner

Now we come to the specific maras. Here we have Outer Maras, Inner Maras, and Secret Maras. There are six Outer Maras:

The Six Outer Maras

1. The Mara of Aversion and Attachment

This is essentially attachment to your near and dear ones, and aversion or hatred towards people and things you do not like. As it is an 'outer' mara, it includes outer circumstances. We are too attached to some people, and have too much aversion to others, and because of this we cannot practise. We become too involved and too tied up in these mind states and cannot move out of this restricted situation. We become bound by the situation and feel we have to work for our near and dear ones, and we have to work against our enemies - to entrap them or avoid them.

Patrul Rinpoche teaches here that *depa* - a strong and stable faith - is important to counter this. *Depa* means more than simply 'faith'; it also includes inspiration, aspiration, and certainty, these three things. When you are inspired by the teachings, you feel a very strong and clear aspiration; you know what your purpose is, what you want to do and how you want to be. You can be certain of your priorities and about how to progress. When you are certain about your path the mara of aversion and attachment cannot become an obstacle. That is the first outer mara.

2. The Mara of Evil Spirits

Here Patrul Rinpoche talks about negative forces that would like to stop you practising Dharma diligently. Sometimes your mind may become a little bit unstable, uncomfortable and unfocussed – 'up in the air' - and you cannot settle on the practice or the meditation. Sometimes you may become ill – all kinds of negative things can happen from different sources.

On such occasions, it could be that negative forces are deliberately coming to harm you, in order to stop you doing anything positive. To counter that, he says the best practice is to meditate on generating loving kindness and compassion. In addition, dedicating tormas to the evil spirits or doing the practice of wrathful deities can also be helpful sometimes.

There are many examples of things like this in the life story of Milarepa [see *The Life of Milarepa*] and other similar biographies. And the kind of things that are described there do happen sometimes, but maybe not so much to people like us, maybe only to very 'high' practitioners.

The text says that these kinds of negative forces can create discord between you and your teacher, between you and your friends and between you and your sponsors. They also create certain kinds of mental states and emotions so that you lose interest in your practice. Unfounded rumours can spread in your name and different kinds of false accusations may spread about you. All these things can happen because of these negative forces. That is what this mara is about.

When this happens, the most important thing to do is to have strong faith, and become very stable and one-pointed. You must become very patient and understand that this is a mara, this is an obstacle, and you should not waver from the practice.

It is usually said that when you go somewhere to try and practice, you should try to make the spirits in that place happy. You should make friends with them all – with the spirits of the mountains, the spirits all around and all the beings there. The principal way to deal with negative forces is compassion. Actually not only here, but in dealing with any kind of negative force or person, compassion is supposed to be the strongest remedy.

The Gyalpo and the Power of Compassion

This is said to be a true story (although I do not know if it is really true myself, but it is said to be). Once upon a time in Tibet, this man and his family were sitting round the fire one evening, when he suddenly said, 'There is somebody calling me!' And then he said, 'Oh yes, yes, okay!' He stood up, went away and didn't come back. Everybody went looking for him. They searched everywhere, near and far, but could not find him.

One month passed, two months, three months ... and then they decided he must be dead and did all the correct ceremonies for forty-nine days. Many months passed, a year passed, and after some time – I don't know how long – he suddenly appeared! He said he had been taken by a gyalpo – one of those Lama demons. This gyalpo had told him many stories.

One story the gyalpo told was about a time he had spotted a big camp of a high Lama and so he had gone to visit it. There were many tents and many monks but he (the gyalpo) had just walked straight through the camp and nobody had seen him. He grabbed a meal here, stabbed someone there – and nobody said anything. Then he went into the central tent where there was an old Lama sitting in meditation posture. This Lama also didn't see him so, very encouraged, the gyalpo just went in and sat on the head of the Lama! - so as to crush him.

Then the Lama started to laugh! He had laughed and laughed and laughed. And as he laughed he became smaller and smaller, until he was almost flat on the seat. The more the Lama laughed, the more the gyalpo wanted to cry; until he cried and cried and was unable to stop crying.

Specific Maras: Outer and Inner 21

The Lama didn't stop laughing, so the gyalpo left – he couldn't take it any more. And the gyalpo said that since that time, for a whole year, he couldn't harm anybody.

The Lama had been meditating on compassion and the gyalpo had been so influenced by that compassion that it prevented him from harming anybody. He simply had no heart to harm anybody after that.

So practising compassion is supposed to be the best way to deal with any kind of negative spirits or ghosts – with anything negative. There are many stories, along similar lines, that demonstrate this.

3. The Mara of the Spiritual Friend or Teacher who is under the Influence of Maras

This means a bad teacher who has become too much under the power of the maras. It also covers when you have friends who are too affected by maras. Because of the influence of such a teacher or friends, your practice deteriorates and you also start doing non-Dharmic or negative activities.

If you realise you are being harmed or influenced by this kind of a mara, you must try to free yourself from those teachers and friends, in a skilful way. You should try to associate yourself with more positive teachers and friends.

4. The Mara of Distraction by too much Success

This can happen to a person who is very successful in terms of their human endeavours; their efforts and abilities, their possessions and wealth. Everything good comes their way, and everything works out extremely well for them. But because everything has gone so well, they become very busy and involved in many things, so that their mind becomes totally distracted. And because their mind is so busy and so distracted by their worldly success, their own practice and diligence in the practice suffers.

That is the mara of the distraction of too much success. So, unless you can develop a certain kind of stability as a practitioner, you should try not to become too involved in too many activities. You should try not to get distracted and you should distance yourself a little bit from the sources of such distractions. That is the method to work on this mara.

5. The Mara of Too Much Preparation

This is when you might say, 'I must do some Dharma practice - that would be such a good thing to do. But in order to do that, I must get everything ready... I must make sure that I have eaten... that I have the right clothes...' and so on! You spend your life making preparations but very rarely get around to actually doing any practice. You become so attached and so involved and so busy with making arrangements and accumulating things for practice or for doing good things, that you never actually start! That is the mara of too much preparation.

The text points out that if you become like this, you may die before you get round to doing anything! So, instead, you should try to be content with simple things for your practice, not necessarily the best things, so that you can just get on and practise without doing too much preparation.

6. The Mara of Too Much Learning

This is the problem of knowing too many things and being too good at everything. You know medicine, logic, history and many other subjects. You can say effective mantras, you can give blessings and healing; you can make things with your hands, you are a good artist. But you are too skilled, too educated and too over-accomplished so that you are so busy doing all these things that you never really sit down to practice. You cannot study and meditate at once, so therefore, too much study can become a mara.

Patrul Rinpoche says that until you develop stability of the mind, try

Specific Maras: Outer and Inner　23

to hide your positive qualities and skills a little bit. He says you should not show off all your skills too much because then you will spend all your time using them. There is a saying in Tibetan: 'Those who are skilled in talking, become the leaders of people. Those who are skilled with their hands, become the servants of people.' So if you are very competent in many ways, everyone will ask, 'Can you do this for me?' 'Can you do that for me?' You may become almost like a servant. You are not a servant, but it is difficult to say no. So it is important not to show off too many skills unnecessarily.

Most of these outer maras are not necessarily a problem. It is about knowing how to use things properly. And it is important to recognise when they do become a problem and then to deal with them in an appropriate way. This is the understanding of the outer maras. Now we look at the Inner Maras:

The Six Inner Maras

1. The Mara of Ignorance

The mara of ignorance is based in not understanding the nature of your mind. Because you do not understand the nature of your mind and yourself, you hold on to your experience of an ego, an independent ego. This self-clinging is the root cause of samsara and, therefore, all our samsaric suffering. It is very important to understand this, from the Buddhist point of view. Whenever we talk about ignorance, the basic ignorance is the ignorance of not understanding our own nature so that we are too much holding on to a self, to an ego. This creates self-centredness.

The remedy is to try and study and reflect and meditate on the teachings on emptiness - *shunyata* (Sanskrit) - and selflessness. This can help lessen your self-centredness a little, and help you understand the true nature of your mind.

2. The Mara of the Mind Poisons, the Kleshas

These are the mind poisons or the afflictive emotions we talked about earlier. This arises when you don't know how to manage these negative emotions; you become under the power of hatred, greed, jealousy and so on. All your positive sides and your positive actions are destroyed by these negative emotions, so you commit negative actions and develop negative habitual tendencies. This will bring you deeper into samsara and, not only deeper into samsara, but deeper into the lower realms. For example, if you have too much hatred or anger then you will experience the hell realm; too much greed can turn you into a hungry ghost. This is the kind of thing we mean by the lower realms.

These are among the strongest maras and, in order to work on them, you need to find remedies and ways to manage your negative emotions. [See, for example, *Dealing with Emotions* Heart Wisdom book]

3. The Mara of Too Much Sensitivity

When you are too self-centred and self-cherishing, you can become over-sensitive: Whatever happens, or whatever is done, you feel it affects you and you take it all too personally. If anyone does anything, or says anything, you feel, 'They deliberately did that to me!' or 'They are talking about me!' We all know someone like this! But, if you are like that, you will have a lot of trouble.

This mara makes your life too full of expectation and you will experience much aversion. The solution is try to be a little bit less sensitive and less clinging and grasping onto your body and mind: not saying 'me, me, me!' too much.

4. The Mara of Laziness

'Laziness' is not a complete translation of this mara. The Tibetan explains that, while you can be too sensitive, you can also be completely insensitive: 'laid back' perhaps or 'not caring.' You have too much inertia and carelessness. It means you do not have much mindfulness, and what you have is too loose or too rarely applied. You are too easily distracted, so you gossip and run around here and there. You take everything too lightly and make it too unimportant. Then, you don't have much self-confidence; you are a little bit sleepy and lazy and 'can't do anything'. All your time goes by without doing anything purposeful and therefore your precious human life is wasted.

In order to overcome this, it is important to develop mindfulness and try to generate diligence and joy in doing more positive things.

5. The Mara of Doubt and Being in Two Minds

This is being uncertain, or lacking a clear confidence in your practice and your understanding, so you are left at a crossroads all the time. You don't know which way to go; your mind is in two minds – 'Shall I do this? Or should I do that?' 'Yes?... no... yes?... no...,' like that. With this mara you have no determination and no clear direction. And without a clear direction and concentrated effort, you won't get any results. The direct translation is 'the mara of two minds.'

The text says that if you are like that, the way to overcome it is to ask your teacher what to do and clarify the situation in that way – provided your teacher is not a 'lazy Lama'![1] You can follow the example of great masters and read *namtars* – the Tibetan word for a biography of a great master is *namtar*. It means the story of their liberation; how that person practised, what they experienced and how they became liberated. If you study these, and take one as an example, then you will know what to do.

6. The Mara of Dualistic Delusion

This refers to understanding everything in an overly concrete way: seeing things as very solid and very 'real,' in a fixed way. It arises because of being in a dualistic state of mind, which is a deluded state of mind. It means that you cannot understand the two truths [i.e. 'Relative Truth' and 'Ultimate Truth,' see Questions and Answers]. The two truths become too separated in your mind, so that you cannot even get onto the path of enlightenment. You become very deluded and your mind becomes very grasping. You see everything as separate and concretely existing, rather than being relative and interdependent.

To work on this, we should meditate in order to come to the right view, a non-dualistic view, and then we can meditate on that.

These are the six maras known as the 'Inner Maras'. They are called the Inner Maras, because they arise through our own way of looking at things and our own emotions. Because of our negative karma, our wrong view and our wrong way of relating to things, these kinds of maras arise and become obstacles on our path. It is important to try to recognise these Inner Maras when they arise and try to find the right remedies - and then to get rid of them!

Specific Maras: Outer and Inner 27

Questions and Answers

Chöd practice

Student: Can you tell us about Chöd practice?

Rinpoche: Chöd is a 'cutting through' practice. First, there is bringing out the negative side, or the attachment and aversion, and then there is cutting through it, cutting it away. In the context of Chöd, we use the word *lhong-tse*, which means something like 'to awaken' - 'to bring out all the problems, to wake them up or disturb them.' You need to bring out the problems because only then do you have the chance to cut through them. That is the idea.

So, when people do the Chöd practice, most people feel at least some fear. We all have fear; we all have attachment and all sorts of other negative aspects. Some people have more of one thing and others have more of another, but fear is the main problem as it is a root cause of all our negativities. Ignorance is the deepest root cause and then, after that, comes fear: the expression of all our mind poisons comes from fear. Anger comes from fear; attachment comes from fear; jealousy and even arrogance all come from fear. Fear is the root cause we need to cut through.

We all have fears, but sometimes when everything is pleasant and going smoothly, we are not aware of them: 'Oh I have no fear!' But only when you actually have to confront something will you know whether you have fear or not. You may be able to face things which are not so bad, but when something really deep or strong happens, then that is the real test, whether you can still handle it then, or not. The thing that brings that about is *lhong-tse* or 'stirring up.' Then *tsar-tse* is when you are able to cut through that.

28   *Specific Maras: Outer and Inner*

Reciting and writing out texts

Student: In the past, students would spend a lot of time reciting texts and writing them out laboriously by hand; and learning texts like the Heart Sutra or the Bodhicharyavatara by heart. Do you think this is still a good practice for us to do nowadays?

Rinpoche: It used to be the custom to do this and, yes, I think it is still a good practice to do. But it was done mainly at a time when there was no printing. Every copy of any text had to be written down by hand. So anything written became very important; writing itself was very important. Maybe now it is less important, because texts can be printed and anyone can easily photocopy them. You can even scan or download texts nowadays, so writing is not so essential in this way.

But it is very good to learn texts, and maybe recite them. I think it is a good exercise to write out a text, especially in nice calligraphy. One woman I know in the South of England is writing out The Lotus Sutra in calligraphy, and then painting it, like the Book of Kells. Her work is so beautiful. She has been working on it for eight years now and needs another eight years to complete it, and sometimes she is working for four to five hours a day! In the end it will be about sixteen volumes!

I know one person in Sikkim who wrote out the whole Prajnaparamita Sutra – all eighteen volumes, in large lettering, just by himself. This would have been normal practice in Tibet. They used to write with gold and silver and all sorts of other things. Before the time of printing the only way was to write things by hand. And I think that is good: you are concentrating so clearly, your mind is wholly on the task and you don't think too much. At one time I also did this. I wrote my first book in Tibetan by my own hand, and many more books besides, and then had them printed and published.

Depa: faith - inspiration, aspiration and certainty

Student: I am very interested in this issue of *depa* and faith; and I am interested also in understanding the concept of hope and how it is incorporated into Buddhist practice. Is there any concept of hope within this idea of *depa*?

Rinpoche: I think so. As we said there are three aspects, or stages, within *depa*. The first is called *dangway depa*. I think there is some sense of hope in this, because it is about when you see or read something, you come across something and it kind of 'rings true'. Your mind is inspired, and maybe that is like finding some hope: 'Yes, it really is like that!' You are no longer feeling lost or hopeless – you are inspired. You have found something convincing, something that rings true and something that can be done. This is the aspect of 'inspiration' as part of *depa*.

The next aspect is 'aspiration'. This contains even more hope, because it means that I see some quality there, something that inspires me and, seeing this possibility or hope, I sincerely want to do something to realise it. So this second part of *depa* includes hope, but it is even more than hope because it includes seeing the possibilities.

The last aspect, the highest, or deepest, kind of *depa*, is 'certainty.' When you have certainty your mind is clear, you have more trust and more clarity. So this is the real *depa*. It is like 'trust' but not a blind or helpless kind of trust, trusting because you have no other choice. You really *know* - not only through intellectual understanding, but deep in your heart, you know: 'Yes, that is it.' There is a deep certainty and clarity; this is the true *depa*.

The nature of time

Student: I have been trying to understand the nature of reality in terms of past, present and future, to understand truly this precious present moment. But for some time now, I have been struggling with understanding the nature of time. Can you direct me towards some sort of clarity? I have understood from teachings before that there is no past and no future. But if there is no past and no future, then does time really exist? But if time doesn't exist, then what is this now?

Rinpoche: I think that when you describe time as past, present and future it is from an experiential point of view, isn't it? Otherwise, what are you calling the present? 'Present' is something that somebody experiences. Time is an experience. Any description or definition of time is based on experience. So when I say, 'This is the present!' I am talking about my own experience. And when I say this is the present, then whatever experience I had, is 'past', and whatever will happen in the future, is 'future'. It is all, therefore, relative.

There is nothing inherent in time that can be called 'present' or 'future' or 'past'. There is nothing 'out there'. There is only experience. Time is measured from an experiential point of view, especially when we talk about past, future and present – there is no way to do otherwise! So, therefore, 'past' is a description or a concept of what happened before 'now'. 'Future' is what might happen after this. And 'present' is the experience that is now. It is my experience. It is anybody's experience. And somebody, yesterday, also experienced the present, a 'now'. So time is a completely relative thing, because it is talking from an experiential point of view.

There is a famous line: 'Past is what has happened; future is what will happen; but how long is the present?' Where is the 'present'? 'Present' is not something that you can find. You cannot find it because as soon as you identify a moment, it is already past. And the next moment, again - past.

Specific Maras: Outer and Inner   31

Whenever you try to catch the present, the 'real' present, it isn't there!

Student: I know Shantideva said the nature of things is like that, but I didn't realise it also applied to time.

Rinpoche: Everything is like that, everything. That is the main point. Time is like that. Nature is like that. Also from the point of view of quantum physics, it is like that. Whenever you try to grasp the 'real thing' you find there is nothing there, nothing to grasp. This is the whole point: it is there but it is also not really there. The fact that it is there is what we call the Relative Truth. Whereas, the true nature of things, that they are also 'not really there', not as a solid entity - when we look for them we cannot find them – that is what we call the Ultimate Truth. Something is there; we can experience it. When it is past, we *did* experience it. We can experience it as if it is future or present, but when we look hard and ask where is it? ... we cannot find it.

Student: So it is appearance and emptiness?

Rinpoche: Yes, it is appearance and emptiness!

All sentient beings

Student: The objects of our practice, those we wish to be benefitted ultimately, are all sentient beings in the Six Realms. Does that include those in the bardo after death?

Rinpoche: Of course. 'All sentient beings' means all sentient beings. Talking about the Six Realms is one way of describing all sentient beings but there are other ways. The important thing is that it encompasses all sentient beings, everywhere, in all realms.

Lamas, Tulkus and rebirth across cultures

Student: I have been trying to understand the role of the Lama, or teacher, in terms of culture. For example, with rebirth, does it have to be that the Lama is always reborn within the Tibetan culture? Is there any possibility that it could be otherwise, especially with cultures mixing more these days? Is it to do with karma?

Rinpoche: There is nothing to say a Lama has to be reborn as Tibetan, not from the Buddhist point of view, or from the Tibetan point of view. From a Buddhist point of view, a Tibetan can be reborn English; an English person can be reborn Tibetan. Not only that, but a human being can be reborn an animal; an animal can be reborn a human being. A human being can go to hell; a human being can be in heaven. You can be reborn in all different kinds of places and not only here in this world, on this globe, but you can be born somewhere totally different, very far away, absolutely anywhere. It is like that.

But in regard to Lamas? Well, first: there is nothing called 'Lamas'! From the Buddhist, or Tibetan, point of view, there is nothing called 'the Lamas' existing separately. And a Lama can be reborn all sorts of different things. There is a particular story where a Lama is reborn as a donkey. But if he/she behaves even worse, he/she can go to lower realms or he/she can become a negative spirit like a gyalpo. He/she can go to the hell realm; he/she can go to heaven; he/she can go anywhere. 'She' can become 'he', 'he' can become 'she' or 'it' – anything like that.

A good Lama - and a 'good Lama' means a good Bodhisattva - can be reborn anywhere. There is no rule that they have to be reborn Tibetan. In respect of Bodhisattvas, it is necessary that they are everywhere, not only everywhere in human societies, but also everywhere in other realms too. Otherwise they cannot fulfil their full use.

However, only the Tibetans have this strange custom, or tradition, of recognising the reincarnations of their high Lamas. It is not done in

Specific Maras: Outer and Inner 33

other parts of the Buddhist world. It developed from the time of the first Karmapa, whose reincarnation was the first formal recognition of this kind.

The first Karmapa, Dusum Khyenpa, was a great master, a highly realised being. His teacher said to him once, 'There are three places you must go: Kham, Tsang and Tsurphu. You should make these three places your main centres and this will bring great benefit in the future.' So he started building monasteries in two of the places but it was not until he was in his eighties that he said, 'I must go to central Tibet now, to near Lhasa. My teacher told me to start some kind of monastery there.' And everybody said, 'Ah, you are too old! You can't go there.' But he said, 'I have to go anyway!' And he went.

He built a small stone hut there, just big enough to sit inside in lotus posture. It was not a very nice place actually. It was very cold, very high up and did not have a good view. But he stayed there until he died. Just before he died he told his students, 'Because my teacher told me I had to build a monastery here, I shall come back as a human being. So please look after my hut, don't let everything be dismantled, and keep all these books carefully because I shall need them when I come back.' And then he died.

After a few years, a boy appeared and said, 'I am Karmapa!' No one took much notice at first. But it turned out that he was a very special boy with great power and he could perform miracles, so he became quite well known. A few years later the Kublai Khan invited the great Sakya Lama, Sakya Pandita, to come and give him teachings. According to Marco Polo the Kublai Khan called a kind of conference of all different faiths, including Christians, Muslims and Buddhists. Sakya Pandita was among those invited and he asked Karmapa to come with him. Then the Kublai Khan asked all the religious leaders to perform a miracle. On the Buddhist side, Sakya Pandita asked Karmapa if he could do something. Karmapa made the cup on the Emperor's table rise up unaided and go to the Khan's mouth so he could drink and then return back down to the table.

So this second Karmapa, named Karma Pakshi, became very famous in Mongolia and China and many students gathered around him. But alas, he didn't do everything that the Kublai Khan asked of him, so he fell out of favour and was put in prison. Then they threw him into the river, but he didn't drown. They tried many ways to harm or kill him, but all failed. In the end they hanged him up by his beard, and that was unbearable! Karma Pakshi called out in pain to Mahakala, his protector, 'Mahakala, please help me! I am in agony!' And he was released but vowed: 'From now onwards, no Karmapa may have a beard!' Since then all the Karmapas have been clean shaven.

When the second Karmapa died, one of his students made sure this was known all over Tibet. Another student, Orgyenpa, recognised the third Karmapa: When a pregnant lady came to see him, he said, 'The child you are carrying is my teacher Karmapa. So take care! When he is born, I shall look after him.' The child was reciting *Om mani pémé hung* in her womb and when he was born he was quite special. He could remember everything and even, later on, wrote an autobiography of his experiences in his mother's womb. This book still exists.

This was the first incident of someone being recognised by a third person as a particular reincarnation. And he became the third Karmapa. Since then, most of the Karmapas have actually written down information where their next rebirth would take place and have been recognised accordingly. Slowly a tradition has grown around this. So when a great Lama, like the Dalai Lama, died, his students would look for his incarnation.

Then this approach started to be applied more widely so that, not only the Dalai Lama and Karmapa were recognised in this way, but it would be very common for search parties to be sent out to find many other lesser Lamas also. If a Lama is a good Lama and builds a monastery

Specific Maras: Outer and Inner

or has many students, when he dies the students say, 'Oh we must find him!' Sometimes they find the right person; sometimes they find the wrong one. It is even possible that sometimes they deliberately put the wrong one into the position because the right one, the real reincarnation, could not do the job!

Student: So is it possible that someone could be reincarnated as a Tulku but not be Tibetan?

Rinpoche: Yes, it is, certainly. There are many examples of this already. The much-loved Gelugpa Lama Thubten Yeshe was reborn in Spain, for example. Before that, the 16th Karmapa recognised one of the Sangyé Nyenpa incarnations in America. That was very strange, and very convincing:

The former Sangyé Nyenpa Rinpoche was a very high Lama and a very good Lama. He was the younger brother of Dilgo Khyentse Rinpoche and he died in Sikkim - we were there. After some years, Karmapa said, 'Oh, he has been reborn somewhere in the West, maybe in America.' He then drew a map and wrote relevant descriptions, and gave it to Sister Palmo, formerly Mrs Freda Bedi, saying, 'This is where he has been born. Find this place!' She tried all sorts of places but it was just a small section of map and was not very specific. It did not give much information and yet the possibilities – 'somewhere in the West, maybe America' - were very large and very wide. She searched and searched but got nowhere.

Then, after many years, they were travelling around America and one day they noticed that the place where they were tallied exactly with the map! There were some place names included on the map. So they looked around and found a very unusual small boy. H.H. Karmapa recognised the boy as Sangyé Nyenpa. He was taken to Rumtek monastery in Sikkim, Northern India, to be educated and he flourished and became really great. Karmapa also recognised another Sangyé Nyenpa in Bhutan, and he was equally as good. Both of them were educated together and it seemed

36   *Specific Maras: Outer and Inner*

very good at the time. But the mother of the American Sangyé Nyenpa had a problem with the arrangement and took him away. He didn't finish his education and I don't know where he is now – somewhere in America probably.

Student: Do Tulkus need any special education in order to do their work?

Rinpoche: If they are to continue in the same kind of traditions as their lineage, then yes, I think special training is necessary. But there are many Tulkus and Bodhisattvas in many different places and different walks of life and they don't need any special 'Tulku training' for what they are doing.

38

Specific Maras: Secret and Top Secret

Now we come to the third category of maras: the Secret Maras. They are called 'secret' because they appear to be somewhat positive, but they are not – they are maras! These are more 'hidden' or 'disguised' or 'obscure' maras. The Tibetan word, *sangwa* means 'secret' or 'hidden.'

The Six Secret Maras

1. The Mara of Sectarianism

It is a mara when you are so strongly attached to your own views and philosophies and so deeply committed to them that you look down on other schools and traditions, and separate yourself from them. This is a sectarian attitude.

2. The Mara of Pride

An example of this mara is when you think you understand the philosophy of, say, emptiness. And because you have mastered such a deep and profound philosophy you become proud of yourself. Because of that pride, you insult or look down on other people and other teachings. You may have some true understanding but you become proud instead of developing the full understanding and your pride thus becomes a mara.

3. The Mara of Scattered Understanding

Your understanding is too much of an intellectual exercise, too conceptual: too much 'in the mouth', only in the words. You know the words very well, you talk a lot, you know all about everything, but you have no experience of what you talk about. So, although you have plenty to say about everything, your experience is superficial and your reactions are no different from the average person. The Tibetan word used here is *chalwa*, which means 'no direction' or 'scattered.' Your understanding is too fragmented, and too much rooted in academic understanding.

4. The Mara of Too Much Expectation

The 'expectation' here is expecting signs of achievement too strongly. You really want, you really expect, some sign of achievement. You long for this so much that you invent it and say, or feel, you have had visions of yidams or something like that, even if you haven't. You might say, and even convince yourself, that you have had an experience of clairvoyance: you feel you should have done, you expected it so much, but actually you didn't really have such an experience. This is too much expectation of the results of practice and is a mara.

5. The Mara of Blind Faith

This is when you don't really understand the practices, but you still want to do them. Because you have a kind of blind faith, you sink yourself into practice before you even know how, like starting a three-year retreat before you have any understanding of even the preliminary practices. And you don't want to study and learn and find out more. Is 'blind faith' the right words for this?

Student: 'Blind faith' is when you believe in something without question and without examining it.

Student: Does it include some aspect of trust, 'blind faith'?

Rinpoche: The Tibetan here is not quite 'blind faith' exactly. *Depa* is faith, which we talked about earlier. The word used here, however, is *lö-dum* which is a 'cut off' kind of 'stupid faith', not ready to study and not even wanting to. That is the mara.

6. The Mara of Misguided Compassion

This is about the wrong use of compassion. Even if you do not have the qualities to help other beings, through teaching or giving advice, you nevertheless try and teach or give advice. You do this out of compassion, but you do it instead of taking the teaching on yourself and doing your own practice. You are trying to help others prematurely or too early on. You are compassionate but you do not yet have the skills you are trying to use.

Compassion is very good, but the important thing is to use that compassion to do something that would be helpful to others, *that you are capable of doing.* This mara refers to when you try to do something you are not capable of doing yet. Another expression of this mara is teaching people how to practise before you have even done the practice yourself. Only afterwards do you try to do it yourself. This is not the right way to go about things and is not good use of compassion.

Specific Maras: Secret and Top Secret 41

The Six Top Secret Maras

Now comes another set of Secret Maras. These are all to do with the Six Paramitas. You could say they are 'Top Secret' in that they are even more hidden or obscure. Usually we would think that anything to do with the Six Paramitas could only be positive. The Six Paramitas are the path of practice laid out for a Bodhisattva: they are the qualities a Bodhisattva aspires to perfect, in order to help all beings. They are: Generosity, Morality (or Discipline), Patience, Diligence, Meditation and Wisdom. The aim is to practise these to a 'perfected,' a transcendental, level where they are not tainted by attachment or other negative mind states in any way.

Here, Patrul Rinpoche shows how even these very good qualities can have a negative side when they are not practised correctly:

1. The Mara of Giving as a Distraction

Let me describe this mara so you can decide if this title is the right way of saying it: When you are supposed to be practising, meditating and so on, you find instead that you want to give – you want to give teachings; you want to collect materials together and distribute them to help people. Perhaps you may help people but the problem is you are trying to do that when you should be practising and meditating yourself.

It is usually said that 'Your actions should be according to the time.' For example, when you are young or you are a student, you should study. If at that stage you don't study but you try to do something like teaching or starting a particular, big project instead, you end up neither studying nor achieving much on this other level either. Similarly, if you are in a retreat or something like that, your focus should be on meditation and that kind of practice. This mara is about when you do not focus properly - according to the time - but instead you want to do all sorts of other activities. So you end up neither getting the one done, nor the other.

Student: You mean when you don't lay the foundations properly?

Rinpoche: No, not that. When you are not focussing on what you are supposed to be doing. What you are trying to do is something that could be very good, but because you are involved with two things, you are not focussing your effort correctly according to the time, you don't actually achieve anything good.

Student: Do you mean when someone is using 'giving' as a distraction?

Rinpoche: Yes. This mara is when you are giving as a distraction.

Student: Does this mean your actions are premature?

Rinpoche: Not premature exactly, more like 'untimely.'

Student: Is it that 'you want to run before you can walk'?

Rinpoche: A little bit, but not necessarily. It is not exactly that. It is more like 'untimely' action. If your focus is on something like meditating, and it remains on that, then you will get better results. But if, while you are supposed to be doing meditation, you want to do something for others instead, then you will actually do neither properly.

Student: You should stick to the task in hand?

Rinpoche: Yes! This is about the mara aspect of generosity or giving. The Six Paramitas are something that we really do have to practise; they are the main practice of the Bodhisattvas. But this is about giving when it becomes a distraction - when you over-do it at the wrong time. Then it is not right and it becomes a mara, because it becomes an obstacle to your spiritual advancement.

2. The Mara of Discipline becoming Penance

Discipline becomes a mara when it becomes too much like 'penance,' when you are overly strict with yourself. Say you are meditating, for example, or practising in solitude; this mara is when you feel you should be very strict, such that you don't eat, you fast all the time; you don't do this and you don't do that. You are so strict that your meditation goes haywire! Your main purpose is to get your meditation right but you are so strict that your discipline actually undermines your efforts.

Another example is when you become sick but you are too disciplined to take proper care of yourself, to take appropriate medicine or food, to the point where it affects your health. It can even become a risk to your life! The mara aspect of discipline is overdoing discipline.

3. The Mara of Patience becoming Obstinacy

The mara side of patience is being 'stubborn.'

Student: Obstinacy?

Rinpoche: Yes, obstinacy may be a better word. Patience is a good quality, but when you take it to an extreme of patience that is unnecessary, patience that is not helpful, then it becomes a mara.

Student: Is it about being over-tolerant?

Rinpoche: It is not quite just being over-tolerant. It is about when you do too much, when you are being so patient in your practice that you expose your body to too much hardship, so that you end up becoming ill. Then you are ill but still you don't go for treatment or do what is necessary to get better - because you are being 'patient.' You are being too passive, just sitting there.

Student: You mean like inertia? That there is a time when one should take action and recognising this is important? You should not let things go on and on when something is wrong?

Rinpoche: Yes, because then you can have an incurable problem and that is no help to anyone. Patience is good but you should not over-do it.

Student: Like things becoming intractable? You are too self-sacrificing?

Rinpoche: Yes, this mara includes when you are self-sacrificing for no reason. There is no usefulness or benefit from your self-sacrifice. It becomes an obstacle to your health and even for your life. So it is an unskilful kind of patience. It is obstinacy rather than patience.

Student: Is it like a 'martyr' type of person?

Rinpoche: Yes, like a kind of 'martyr' maybe. Always trying and trying, but unnecessarily.

4. The Mara of Exhausting Diligence

The Tibetan word for this mara, *tang-che*, means 'burnt out' or 'exhausted.' You are very diligent about something but too much so. You do it too harshly and too severely. You become fed up and exhausted: you are 'burnt out.' Your body cannot take it anymore so after a while you have to give it up. This is a wrong way of being diligent.

5. The Mara of Overemphasis on Stability of Meditation

This is when you become over attached to meditation, overly grasping of meditation itself. You put too much emphasis on letting your mind become peaceful and stable. You just meditate, meditate, meditate. While you do let your mind calm down, you don't actually do anything to liberate it. You don't do any kind of study or use any other means to develop wisdom. All you do is just keep trying to make your mind calm, only ever practising shiné [calm-abiding meditation] – until it becomes a problem. This is an over-emphasis purely on the stability of meditation.

Specific Maras: Secret and Top Secret   45

6. The Mara of Wisdom that Generates Mind Poisons

There is an aspect of wisdom that can actually generate mind poisons instead of getting rid of them. Wisdom is crucial and the means to develop it is through study, reflection and meditation. But a mara can arise when you develop wisdom through these means and that becomes a reason for you to become proud and self-satisfied. You get kind of 'puffed up' and mind poisons creep in: you become proud, you become jealous and so on. The process, instead of helping you get rid of your mind poisons, or afflictive emotions, has actually made you acquire and generate mind poisons.

Student: Is it something like fundamentalism? Or extremism?

Rinpoche: I think fundamentalism is like the first mara here – the mara of sectarianism. This is more a case of: you study, you reflect, you meditate, you understand a bit ... and then you say '*This* is the right thing!' and get over confident. 'I know everything! I am a very wise person! Even my meditation is very good.' And you become very proud. Then you get very angry with anybody who seems to criticise you.

Student: Would you say it includes 'complacency'?

Rinpoche: Yes, I think complacency is part of this. Complacency gives you ego, too much ego.

Student: 'Set up in your own conceit'?

Rinpoche: Yes, 'set up in your conceit' – that's right. So, therefore, some wisdom is there, but that wisdom doesn't help to make you humble. You feel that 'What I understand is right, and the rest is not right,' so you say bad things about other people. And if anyone criticises you even a little bit, you become infuriated and say that nobody else knows anything. This is an example, this mara includes all kinds of things like this.

Patrul Rinpoche says that when this sixth Paramita - *sherab*, wisdom

- becomes corrupted, we must rely on a learned teacher as the antidote, and try to understand things clearly.

How *not* to practise: The story of the Black Cat

So, what Patrul Rinpoche is saying here – and this is the heart of the matter – even the Six Paramitas, if you overdo them, or do them in the wrong way, become maras. We talk about 'The Middle Way' or 'The Middle Path' and it is very important. Also, it is important from the Buddhist point of view: any practice or any instruction should not be done just for the sake of doing it – that's not the point, that's not the purpose we practise.

The main reasons to consider when doing any practice are:

Firstly, whether it is really working for the benefit of people.

Secondly, whether it is helping your samsaric state of mind.

If it is not helping either of these then, even if it is supposed to be the highest meditation or the most important philosophy or the deepest wisdom, it is useless. It is not even just useless – it is a mara! That is the understanding.

If we understand this clearly, then we will not have a problem with our practice. People can sometimes become a little too rigid about their practice, especially when they don't know that much: 'Yes, this *has* to be done because my Lama said so. It *has* to be done and it has to be done *like this*! If I don't do this then it is *not right*.' And it becomes like the black cat story. You know the black cat story? It is my favourite story...

A teacher and his students used to meet in their centre and meditate together in the evening. Now, this teacher had a black kitten which played about and disturbed people during their meditation. So they made a rule that when people came in for the meditation, they would first tie up this kitten, then sit down and do the practice. When they had finished they would untie the kitten and go away.

Specific Maras: Secret and Top Secret   47

So this went on month after month, year after year. Then, after many years, the teacher passed away and his best student became the teacher and the whole thing continued. They came in, tied up the cat, sat for the meditation, untied the cat, and left. One day, the cat also died of old age.

'How', they said, 'How can we do the meditation now because we have no cat to tie up?'

'It is necessary to come in and tie up the cat before we practise! And then when we have finished, we untie the cat!'

But now they had no cat to tie up.

So they tried to find a cat exactly like the one who had died, a completely black cat without a single spot. They went all over the city, all over the surrounding countryside, to find a completely black cat without a spot. Finally, after much difficulty, they found one. They brought the cat to the centre, tied it up, sat for their meditation, and then untied the cat.

It is not difficult to become like that. But that is a mara. And the advice is to be careful not to become like that!

Patrul Rinpoche explains that when these Six Paramitas become maras it is like a medicine that starts to have side effects, side effects that can poison you. Even the Paramitas can become maras, obstacles on the path. So it is important to try and understand these maras, to examine them and then to try and get rid of them. In essence, whatever harms the progress of a practitioner and becomes an obstacle to liberation, to freedom, is regarded as a mara. We need to recognise the maras and get rid of them!

Questions and Answers

Negative forces

Student: A lot of the discussion about maras seems to include states of mental illness. In the past it was sometimes thought that negative spirits, or suchlike, took possession of a person, to cause deep-seated problems. Now we might see that in a more psychotherapeutic way, for example, people having addiction problems or problems coming from difficult circumstances early on in their life or on-going in their everyday life. Does that mean that the antidotes for these problems or maras will include psychotherapeutic approaches?

Rinpoche: Let us wait until we come to the section where the antidotes are given and then see. We have already described the meaning of the maras - things that obstruct! This will not always be like being possessed by an evil spirit or something like that. But a certain kind of harm from certain kinds of negative forces is not discounted. However, when we talk about a 'negative force' from the Buddhist point of view, it does not necessarily have to mean a 'being.' It can be many different things.

Maras and karma

Student: Are maras affected by karma?

Rinpoche: Yes, but karma is always present: there is nothing that is not affected by karma. Karma is your whole experience. Karma is there anyway. But karma is not something 'un-changeable.'

Student: In particular situations can our karma be brought out? Like negative karma ripening much faster, maybe due to a particular practice? Is this part of mara?

Rinpoche: This will come later on so maybe I shouldn't say much about that here. But the practice of dharma is to bring the obstacles onto the path, and transform them into accomplishment. Transforming the mara into accomplishment, this is the main practice. So, the question is how to do that? - With wisdom, with compassion, and with other means. It is not, 'Ugh! This is a mara!' It is not like that. We have to bring the mara onto the path and transform it, transform the negative into the positive. How much we can manage that is the whole point. But we shall discuss this more later.

Whose mara?

Student: You were talking about situations where someone might suddenly be abandoned, or people might give you a poor reputation, or hate you for no reason, and that these are maras. But I am not sure whether they would be their maras, or my maras or both together?

Rinpoche: In such a situation it would be your mara. Yes, definitely your mara.

Student: I don't understand. If this is my mara, how did I create it?

Rinpoche: You did not necessarily create it but it is an *obstacle* for *you*.

Purelands and 'blind faith'

Student: I have a question about the 'mara of blind faith.' We say prayers to be born into a Pureland. But I can't see how we can gain conviction that there is a Pureland, except by blind faith? It feels different to other aspects of Dharma study like logic, contemplation and experience.

Rinpoche: 'Pureland' is not only about blind faith. 'Pureland' is a practice. We talk about the four practices of the Pureland. If you follow these four practices, you will be born into the Pureland of Amitabha. Now what are these four things?

1. Generating Bodhicitta.
2. Doing positive things, many positive things.
3. Always thinking of, or focussing on, the Pureland. This means focussing on pure qualities and seeing the pure side of things.
4. Praying to be reborn in Dewachen [the Tibetan name for the Pureland of Amitabha] and focussing your mind on Buddha Amitabha.

This is quite a good practice, because if you are generating Bodhicitta that means you have some compassion and wisdom. You are concerned for all sentient beings and want to do positive things for them. By generating Bodhicitta, you will become a Bodhisattva.

Then, in addition, your mind will be concentrated on the Pure Realm, the positive side, and not distracted by negative things. Your mind will not be filled with either aversion or attachment. You will always be thinking of Amitabha Buddha; you will be praying to be reborn in Dewachen.

Thus your mind will always be concentrated on something pure and positive. So all the practice you need is there. Whether you will be immediately born there or not – that's another story! But I think it is a very good and positive practice, and it is simple and straightforward in a way too.

Student: Rinpoche, wouldn't that be against the Bodhisattva Vow to focus on being reborn in a Pureland? Shouldn't you be focussing helping all beings?

Rinpoche: Yes, yes, you should. But your being born into a Pureland is not obstructing you from working for the benefit of other beings. Your being born into the Pureland is actually helping you to work for the benefit of other beings.

Student: Can you come back from the Pureland to help other beings?

Specific Maras: Secret and Top Secret 51

Rinpoche: Yes, this is how it is described. You have to first understand what a 'Pureland' is. There are all sorts of 'Purelands' or 'Pure Realms.' If you are born there, you are born out of a lotus flower and will immediately see Buddhas all around you. You will no longer be in a samsaric state of mind; you will already have arrived at a realised state of mind, at one of various different stages.

You will always be able to see what is happening in the world 'down there' - the human realm, the animal realm, every realm. You would be able to go and visit all other Buddha Realms if you like, including the world we are in here, visit it and return to the Pureland. If you find some of your friends or relatives are dying you can go and bring them back with you to the Pureland. That is how it is actually described.

So, if you decide to be born as a human being, or as an animal, or as whatever – and see someone needing help, you can go there and be there with them for a time and come back again. So it is like a 'base camp!' Sounds very good, no? Yes, I think so!

Spirits

Student: William Shakespeare, the playwright, describes in his plays a kind of special light around a person when they die, and spirits coming around them. Is that something that really happens?

Rinpoche: I don't know if spirits come around when someone is dying; maybe they do. In many Buddhist texts it is said to be beneficial to do certain practices or strong dedications on specific days, such as the solstices, or the equinoxes, or on solar or lunar eclipses, and also on full or new moon – these are said to be powerful times. And usually, from the Tibetan point of view, on the Tibetan calendar, the 9th and the 19th days of the lunar month are powerful, and especially also the 29th day – just before the new moon – is supposed to be the day when many spirits, or beings like spirits, are active. This is why we do Mahakala practice on those days.

But I don't know much about these things. I haven't seen any spirits myself. One time I thought I had such an experience. I was in this very old house, and I was the only one at that time staying there. It was night-time and I had turned off the light and was fast asleep. Then suddenly: 'Click!' - the light came on! I turned it off again, but suddenly, again, it turned back on! And then I heard something, like 'Tuck... tuck ... tuck ...', like somebody walking. I got out of bed, went out and looked down the staircase; I looked everywhere – nothing.

So I turned off the light again and went to back to sleep. Once again: 'Click!' the light came on. So I thought, 'This house must be haunted! I have never been anywhere haunted before, but it must be haunted here.' And I went back to sleep!

The next morning, I asked the landlord, 'Is this house haunted?'

'We don't know. Well, maybe because it is a very old house.'

I said, 'There is something very strange happening because when I turned off the light, it came on again, and again'.

The landlord said, 'Oh! Maybe that was the button behind the cupboard!'

There was a cupboard behind my bed and there was a light switch just behind that so whenever I turned over or moved my bed a little bit it knocked the switch.

'But I heard somebody walking, like 'Tuck... tuck ... tuck ...'

'Maybe that was the chimney? The house is very old and there is a leak in the chimney so when it rains you can hear the drips.'

So it was like that! The house was not haunted at all. But that is the nearest I have come to experiencing ghosts or spirits.

Specific Maras: Secret and Top Secret   53

Extinguishing desire

Student: I have another question about something else William Shakespeare wrote. He says at the start of one of his plays: 'If music be the food of love, play on! Give me excess of it; that, surfeiting, the appetite may sicken and so die.' His point being, that if you take anything to excess, the desire for it will, of itself, cease. So if you drink too much for example, in the end you just get fed up with it and realise you will be happier without it. Is this approach a remedy for the maras?

Rinpoche: Who has managed this? If there is anyone here who has done something to this kind of excess and can tell us what his or her experience was, please tell us!

Student: Well, Lama Yeshe Losal here in Samye Ling says he spent a long time in New York experiencing everything he could, until he got fed up with it all and came here to spend the rest of his life as a monk!

Student: I have done some things to excess, Rinpoche, certainly in the past. Then I realised that this activity was making me ill. I explored it as far as I could; but it wasn't that I rejected it mentally, it was more that my body rejected it.

Rinpoche: Generally the understanding is that drinking too much, or whatever, does not necessarily satisfy us. There are many instances where people do not say, 'Now I have drunk enough and I am totally satisfied!' Sometimes people get sick, their liver is damaged and they physically cannot drink alcohol any more. But usually when you are addicted to something you want to go on doing it.

Of course you might find after some time that it is not good for you; or for some other reason, you may choose to give it up. Then, if you are strong enough, you may manage to do so. But I know many people who have died of excessive drinking, actually particularly Tibetans. Tibetans are very bad drinkers. They easily get addicted to alcohol and then it is very difficult to get rid of the habit; in too many cases the liver gets wrecked and they die. Maybe some people indulge too much and then say, 'Okay, this is doing no good' and stop; there are people like that. But others will just continue.

Maras in our lives

Student: I am imagining how a life might unfold: A small child will be affected by different kinds of maras, but know nothing about them and not understand why they are in these states of mind. So they have a combination of these symptoms we were discussing. Maybe they start to live their lives always feeling dissatisfied and restless as a result. Later that could develop further into mental disturbances, which could become depression, or addictions could arise. Such a person would easily end up living in a kind of prison, an unhealthy state of dissatisfaction because of being unable to cope.

Is that how it happens? Is that why so many people, including myself at times, have this feeling: 'Why can I not be satisfied?' or 'Why do I have this? Why do I not have that?' I don't know why I am not happy. Do you think it is also to do with maras?

Rinpoche: When you are describing maras like this, I think you are describing them in a very broad way. From this point of view, almost anything that creates obstructions or obstacles to your happiness, to your well-being and your practice of Dharma, is a mara. 'Practice of Dharma' does not mean a religious path here, but more generally any means of bringing lasting happiness to yourself, and solving your problems. So, therefore, yes, this kind of situation could be seen as due to maras.

Of course all of us have these types of problems. The main thing is that we all want to do something good for ourselves but we don't know what will really benefit us and what will not; we are not sure what will be good for the long run and what will not. Gradually, when we do realise a little bit that 'this is not a good thing,' or start to understand 'this is good' and 'this is even better,' then we can become a little wiser.

Sometimes we feel that our happiness comes from wealth, or from fame, or from pleasure, or from power. And then we go after all these four things. When we finally have money or fame or so on, we may find we have had to do all sorts of other things which were not very good for us and not very good for others. We get caught up in all sorts of traps and addictions – all sorts of things – until we don't know what is real any more, what really does bring us happiness. Understanding this becomes very important. But it has to be understood in a complete way. It is *not* to say that if you have *no* wealth, *no* power, *no* fame or recognition or pleasure, then you will be happy either. It is not saying that at all.

These four are part of what are called the 'Eight Worldly Dharmas' [see glossary]. The absence of these four are also worldly dharmas. Presence of these four, and absence of these four, together make up the Eight Worldly Dharmas; both having them and not having them. The teaching is not saying we should not have power or fame or wealth or pleasure. It is saying that happiness has to come from within ourselves – and this is something very important to understand. It doesn't mean you don't need any money or should not have any luxuries. To have a few nice things is very pleasant. If you can enjoy them without too much attachment, or too much aversion to their opposite, there is no problem. There is nothing wrong with that. But if you have too much attachment or too much aversion to something, that is what causes problems. It is not the things themselves; it is our way of experiencing them, our way of reacting to them, that causes problems.

The understanding is that we must learn how to experience things in a proper way. It is about learning how to carry ourselves. When someone understands this more deeply then they know how to balance themselves. It is not just about going away to the mountains or completely giving up everything you have; neither is it about getting more and more

56   *Specific Maras: Secret and Top Secret*

things for yourself. It is about learning how to experience things, how to balance your mind.

So when you recognise your obstacles – you can call them maras if you like - when you realise what they are, you can notice when they arise. 'Oh this is a mara coming up.' It means that you are aware of it and therefore don't get totally caught up or lost in it. Then you might realise another mara is coming from another direction, and you become aware of that too. There is also no need to get in a panic about it, 'Oh I am always surrounded by maras!' Again, if you become neurotic about maras this can become a problem in itself! We have to understand all of this in a balanced way - so we make the maras harmless. I think this is the whole point of the teaching. And we will come more specifically to the remedies later.

58

The Causes of Maras and their Activities

Now Patrul Rinpoche describes the main reasons why maras happen: their source or their causes. He says that maras will arise:

- *If you don't practise diligently, if you are lazy*
- *If you have too little understanding, or too little intelligence*
- *When your mind poisons are too strong*
- *If you have too many rambling thoughts, or your mind is too busy*
- *If you have too many ideas, too many thoughts of 'I could do this... or this...'*
- *If you don't have a good, authentic teacher*
- *If you don't have or don't receive deep instructions*
- *If you have negative friends or companions*
- *If you cling to anything too much*
- *If you have too much desire, or too much lust*
- *If you like meat and drink too much*

Student: When you say 'drink,' do you mean 'intoxicating drink'?

Rinpoche: Oh yes, not just orange juice!

Maras will arise:
- *If you are constantly changing your mind, your mind is too fickle*
- *If you are too stubborn and nothing can change you*
- *If you are arrogant or proud*
- *If you are a beginner practitioner and like solitude too much*
- *If you like the town and cities too much*
- *If you live in a place, or area, with people you don't like, or who don't like you*
- *If you take on too many commitments or start too many practices that you cannot fulfil*
- *If you don't have real, deep instructions, but try to practise without them anyway, out of obstinacy, although you don't know how to do the practice properly*
- *If your mind is too unstable so you don't stick to the commitments you have made.*
- *If you take dreams too seriously, that is also a source of mara*

Student: Dreams?

Rinpoche: Yes, like if you have a good dream and you take it too seriously – or if you have a bad dream, also taking it too seriously. You should not give too much importance to dreams.
- *If you like signs and omens too much – that is also a source of mara*
- *If your mind becomes less confident, or you lose confidence*

Student: Losing self-confidence?

Rinpoche: Yes, you feel 'Oh, I can't do anything!' You lose your confidence.

Student: You put yourself down?

Rinpoche: Yes, you lose self-confidence or self-esteem ...

Student: Losing faith in your ability?

Rinpoche: Losing faith in your ability, yes, that's it. Losing faith in your abilities and also finding that your mind is unhappy and unsettled, that is also a sign of mara. So, therefore, whenever you find any of these things happening, try to examine them and try to do something to get relief, to get out of that situation.

Student: It looks, to me, like these are all normal things that might happen due to our past. We cannot avoid them happening. So, to realise these things are happening and then do something about them is quite hard. Sometimes we are bound to lose faith, or be distracted.

Rinpoche: Yes, that is what I'm saying. When you notice these things are happening, you must say, 'This is an obstacle! This is a mara!'

Student: But surely they are unavoidable? That is what I cannot fathom.

Rinpoche: Yes, that is true. That is why Patrul Rinpoche is saying that you should not expect your path to be free of things like this. You should not expect that your path will be a certain way - that it will be completely smooth and problem-free. You should not expect that to be the case. There will be many hurdles, many maras, and many things to challenge you.

And all these things we have mentioned can, of course, happen to anybody – that is what Patrul Rinpoche is saying. And when they happen, you have to be alert and notice that something is not right and try to prevent it going further.

When you feel, 'Oh, I have no ability! I cannot do that!' - at that point you have to realise it is not the case, that it is just an obstacle arising. When you understand that, you will know it is wrong and also it is not something solid. Then you might start thinking, 'Oh I have all the abilities! I can do anything!' And you need to notice that idea is also an obstacle – you know that that is not true either. When you get both these attitudes in balance then you are okay.

This is all about how to take life – all these things are just about life.

They are nothing special. All practice is about how to be a better person; how to be able to look after yourself; how to do something that is good for you and good for others. That is the whole thing in a nutshell.

The most important thing is that when the ups and downs come, we should not think, 'That's it, I cannot do anything!' or 'Oh, I'm unhappy! I am the lowest, the dregs. I can never be happy. I shall be always like this.' And then wallow in the unhappiness. Somehow everybody knows in a way that that is not the case. You may be very unhappy today, but tomorrow perhaps, or maybe after a few days, you will be happier. So, therefore, you should truly try to understand that this is just an obstacle. It is not something that is there all the time, but you will have to do something to get rid of it. Maybe you only have to relax to counteract it, and then things will sort themselves out.

Continuing with the main reasons why maras happen - their source and their causes - Patrul Rinpoche says that maras will arise:

- *If you take on students who are not suitable or who don't have the right attitude or aptitude.*
- *When the teacher and the student don't share the same views and don't agree on the right action to take, but they still try to work together!*
- *If you work too hard on studies and reflections that don't help you, that don't take you along the path.*
- *If you make too much effort where there is no need; there is no result and no meaning to it.*
- *If you rely on friends who are only interested in profits and fame, who are too desiring or too ambitious.*
- *If you collect followers and teach Dharma out of your own pride and arrogance, rather than because you want to help people.*
- *If you try to be a teacher to others even though you don't have the right*

education or qualities yourself.

- *If you say you take refuge in the Buddha, Dharma and Sangha but you have no faith or devotion. You personally have no inspiration, aspiration or certainty, but just go along with it because that is what everybody else is doing.*
- *Being happy to teach others before you have any understanding yourself is an activity of mara.*

However, I often encourage people to share their knowledge, even if they don't know very much. The example I give is of a teacher who once said, 'I taught my students and I explained everything, and they didn't understand. And then I explained it a second time, even more carefully, in even more detail, but still they didn't understand. When I explained it for the third time, finally, *I* understood!' Sometimes it happens like this. I usually say that teaching is a good way of learning, maybe the best way of learning, but perhaps it is at the expense of the students!

- *Wanting to have the result as soon as you start to practise is also a mara.*
- *The things you want to do in order to benefit people should not become your livelihood.*

Patrul Rinpoche says here that you should not practise 'medicine, mantra, and other activities for your livelihood.' He does not mean that all doctors should not be doctors! Of course, things were different in olden days. I think for us it means that one should not try to make too much profit out of helping others, otherwise it could become exploiting them.

There is one very great female practitioner, Jamyang Khyentse's Khandro, who came to the West and was invited to teach in many centres. She travelled widely and met many Lamas. At one place she met with Kalu Rinpoche and he asked her, 'How do you find Buddhism is getting on in the West?' And do you know what she said?

The Causes of Maras and their Activities   63

She said, 'I see that the centres are selling the Lamas. And the Lamas are selling the Dharma.' *That* is what we should *not* do!

– *When Dharma practitioners try to live on negative activities or harmful livelihoods, that is the work of maras.*

Traditionally, we talk about the 'five wrong livelihoods' [see glossary]. For example, a wrong livelihood for ordained Sangha is living off what is offered to the Buddha, Dharma and Sangha, or what is not given to you.

– *If you like too much having lots of followers, or you need lots of students, or gain generally, like money.*
– *Even when you know that some things are harmful to your mind, you don't give them up.*
– *If you like worldly entertainment too much* (which means you shouldn't watch too much TV!)
– *If you are always too busy or always going to distracting places.*
– *To use things that generate arrogance and pride too much is also a sign of a mara.* For instance, you think you need to have a very fine horse, lots of ornaments or too good a car – to show off!
– *If you become mindless and careless when you do things.*
– *If you mindlessly overindulge in luxuries, in sex, in eating (particularly meat) and drinking alcohol, or even in too much sleep.*
– *Whatever is inspired by the Eight Worldly Dharmas, or the Eight Worldly Concerns* [see glossary].
– *If you are too active or do too much travelling or even talk too much.*

I am wondering now if Patrul Rinpoche is talking about me!

– *Too much thinking - that is also an activity of mara.*

In essence, whatever is not according to the Dharma - that is, something that helps you and helps others - can be regarded as the activity of mara. The instruction is to lessen them and try to get rid of them.

How to realise you are affected by mara

There are several signs, and ways of realising that you have been affected by a mara. The first is by a general sign, such as the following:

– *Your five mind poisons are more prevalent and stronger than before and things happen because of this. Then you have to realise and understand that you are affected by a mara.*
– *Without any reason you feel tired and your meditation power is decreased.*
– *There are too many kinds of illnesses, or negative incidents, or sudden accidents happening.*
– *Your mind becomes dull and unclear, misty and 'covered'. Mindfulness becomes much less.*
– *Without any reason your mind is uncomfortable, unsettled and unhappy.*
– *You want to die, so that you might even find yourself making arrangements for suicide or something like that.*
– *Without attaining the stage of realisation where you may choose to do so healthily, you want to give away parts of your body, your flesh and blood and things like that to others.*

Student: Does that include giving blood?

Rinpoche: That, I think, is okay. I don't think giving blood is a bad thing to do.

Student: What about donating organs?

Rinpoche: Maybe not too good and not too bad. It depends - I have been told that you can give your liver, and your liver can grow back again. Maybe if it is the right time, and there is a good doctor and it doesn't make you too ill, then it is okay to donate an organ.

Student: Is Patrul Rinpoche saying you should not do certain practices if you are not at a high enough level?

Rinpoche: No, here he is talking about giving away parts of your body for real. I think maybe some people did that – I don't know!

Student: The Bodhisattvas did. There is a story about cutting lumps from their flesh to feed hungry animals.

Rinpoche: Yes, something like that. People have always done all sorts of strange things. People are not only crazy now! They have always been a little bit crazy. I don't think Patrul Rinpoche is talking about donating blood or donating organs here. He is more talking about how you do things, your state of mind. If you are at a certain level of understanding and you give blood, then it is okay; but if you overdo it then it may not be so good.

Student: Sometimes people who are mentally ill do want to hurt themselves quite extremely. It is called 'self-harming.'

The text continues to say:

- *If you are fed up with your body, if you insult your body, your own flesh and limbs without any reason, if you cut and torture your body, it is a sign you are affected by mara.*

Then we have the following signs that you are affected by mara:

- *When your Bodhicitta, your compassion, deteriorates, and you have no patience for Dharma and the practice of Dharma. You have no patience and cannot forbear any hardships at all.*

66   *The Causes of Maras and their Activities*

- *You have lots of wrong views coming up and want to do negative things.*
- *Your confidence in Dharma becomes unstable and you have many doubts about the practice of the Dharma.*
- *Your mind is attracted too much towards worldly gains and luxuries. Your desire for wealth and certain things, objects, becomes too strong.*
- *You find yourself doing all sorts of strange things. Your actions and speech become very strange; you have no shame or shyness and do things like going about naked with no inhibitions or shame.*
- *You become very irritable and short-tempered and are angry with everybody.*

Student: Does that mean that mental illness is a sign that you are affected by maras?

Rinpoche: Yes, sometimes, definitely.

The signs of mara continue:

- *If you become too obsessed with something, whether it is food or drink or sex or anything, so that you think about it day and night and it even comes up in your dreams.*
- *If your mind is very active and very efficient in all worldly things like business or other activities, but is very dull, distracted and lazy in the practice of Dharma or in anything positive to do with yourself and others. Whenever you try to practise, or engage in positive activities, your mind does not settle. When you try to do something with Dharma, instead all sorts of negative things happen.*
- *If your mind is totally fed up with study, reflection and meditation and you become completely discouraged when even small obstacles arise.*
- *If you have dreams that are too good, or too bad, too much up and down.*

- *You don't like staying in one place; you become very restless, and always want to go somewhere else. The minute one negative emotion finishes, another comes up. You become very jealous or arrogant or stingy or full of deep desire. If these things happen it is a sign you are affected by the mara.*
- *You find yourself always praising yourself and criticising others.*
- *You see the Buddha, Dharma and Sangha as being inferior. You see things in a very sectarian way and criticise people. You have no respect for holy beings but always find faults and say bad things about good people.*
- *You like, you enjoy distractions too much. You don't want to meditate - but you do want to teach! You want to use mantra on others and do lots of prayers for other people but you don't want to listen to the teachings. In fact, as soon as you start to listen to a teaching or start to practise, you go to sleep!*
- *Without any reason, fear comes up at night, your heart trembles and you just panic without any cause.*
- *The radiance of your face is decreased – that is also a sign you are affected by mara.*

Student: Rinpoche, are there remedies for any of these?

Rinpoche: I think so. There must be some! Otherwise what is the point?

Student: We all do all these things so, if there are no remedies, we are doomed!

Rinpoche: I think there are some treatments. Maybe just a few. Don't despair just yet. Don't cut off your limbs until we get to the place! We are almost coming to the end of the maras and then there will be some antidotes coming up. One last sign you are affected by mara is:

– *You are falsely accused of baseless allegations; people hate you for no reason and give you a bad name. Friends and sponsors that you have been very close to abandon you without reason.*

We have learned many different signs of being affected by the maras. There are a few more, which we will not look at in detail here. Mainly, these are false signs of achievement: they seem good but they are misleading. For example, having visions of Buddhas and deities, or having some kind of an experience that makes you think you are at a certain level of realisation. These things seem like realisation but they are not, they are just obstacles.

How to know the difference? The main indicator is compassion. When seemingly positive things happen, if you look at your mind and find that it is not any calmer, that your irritability, anger, jealousy, pride and desire are not less – then you have not experienced a sign of realisation. If your mind is strongly affected by the Eight Worldly Dharmas, then you have to say that it is not attainment, it is not realisation – it is mara. If you have no compassion either for yourself or others and no kind of peace and joy, something is wrong. If these things *are* present - peace and joy and compassion - then you can say that there is progress, genuine realisation.

If your mind is full of signs that seem to be positive, and you feel you have attained something good, then you may become too attached to it, or become proud of yourself and things like that. Or if something is unpleasant your mind will feel aversion and fear. In both cases, it is mara. Anything that brings up aversion and attachment is mara.

Now, you will be pleased to hear there are plenty of remedies to come. But I don't know how easy it is to apply them...

Questions and Answers

Does 'the end justify the means'?

Student: One of the phrases you used causes me difficulties. You said that 'the path is the means to an end.' This phrase worries me because it is like the Marxist slogan, 'the end justifies the means.' Is this an appropriate understanding – that the means is an end in itself – just becoming a better person?

Rinpoche: What I meant was that the path is regarded as a 'method.' When we talk about 'path' in Buddhism, the path is a means, a 'method', something that helps you in one way or another to go in a particular direction. The path is not regarded as something absolute but as a skilful means of working on something. From the Buddhist point of view, there is nothing called *'the* (only) right path.' There is what is recommended, but if that is not useful for a particular person at a particular time, it would not be a good path or a good system, for them to follow.

Student: Is that what you meant yesterday, when you said that something negative can end up giving positive results? In Communism, however, that could mean doing something bad in the short term to achieve a long term positive goal. When we start talking about a negative obstacle being good if the end result is good, is that 'the end justifying the means'?

Rinpoche: 'The end justifies the means;' sayings like this depend on how you take them. If you take them in an absolute way then it becomes very difficult. It becomes wrong. That is the whole point we are discussing here.

If you say the end justifies the means and make that something completely rigid, and *always* right, then that is not correct. That becomes a mara! But if you say the end doesn't matter, the means is the most important thing, that also is not correct. That also becomes a mara. This is the Buddhist way of understanding.

We have to be careful about how people understand what we say, of course. But the most important thing to understand from the Buddhist view, is that to make one slogan or doctrine the one and only way to go, like 'that is how it is, and that is that!' – that only creates problems.

Student: To my mind, until we reach enlightenment there is no end point, so therefore it is all means. And that 'end' is the realisation that it is all a process. To say 'the end justifies the means' assumes that you get to an 'end' which retrospectively justifies the means. If there is no end point, the whole path is only a means.

Student: In the West we say, for this, 'the means are an end in themselves.'

Rinpoche: Well, whatever we say, if we say it too strongly, then it will become a problem! That is what this whole teaching shows us. If you say 'the means is the end,' that the 'means' is the only thing that matters, that becomes a problem. And if you say 'the end' is the only thing, and the 'means' do not matter, that too becomes a problem. From the Buddhist point of view, it is interdependent and anything that is done to excess, even the Six Paramitas, is too much. Any excess is not the 'middle way.' That is the main point here. To say that Buddhism says 'the means is the end' or Buddhism says 'the end is the means' – both are wrong; neither is the case.

The clarity of the mind

Student: Can I ask a question about the nature of mind? You have talked sometimes about the clarity aspect of the mind and about how duality arises when we mistake our awareness of that. I have heard the phrase the 'self-clarity of appearance' in connection with this. Could you clarify what this clarity is please?!

And a second question about this is how can we use that clarity in meditation? Is it something we should try to develop an awareness of or is it something that spontaneously arises and then we just have to recognise it?

Rinpoche: From the Buddhist point of view, what I experience is myself, is my mind. Everything I experience happens within my mind so, in a way, it is my mind. So then, if we ask, what is the main aspect in that experience? It is the consciousness. And what is the main aspect of that consciousness? It is awareness. Awareness is the essence of consciousness. Therefore, if I really want to understand my mind, or my consciousness, it is this awareness I need to look at.

So, what is the nature of this awareness? The essence of the consciousness is actually usually called 'clarity'. The meaning of 'clarity' here is not the clarity that comes when you switch on a light and its rays light everything up. It is not that kind of clarity we are talking about here, that makes other things clear. 'Clarity' here means that you are 'aware', you have a sense of awareness. This clarity, in the Buddhist view, is not small – it is vast! It is the potential to be omniscient, to see very clearly about everything and anything.

But the experience of that all-knowing, all-seeing clarity can only happen when your mind becomes freed from all obscuration. The understanding from the Buddhist point of view is that we have the potential to be completely clear with no confusion, knowing almost all about everything and having no doubts. But our mind is not like that at the moment. Our mind is a little bit confused and full of all sorts of unhappiness and sadness and fear and emotions and things like that.

Student: Is that self-clarity of appearance?

Rinpoche: What is self-clarity of appearance? What is the difference?

Student: I don't know. Mingyur Rinpoche mentions it when he talks about clarity.

Rinpoche: Yes, but clarity is clarity. 'Clarity of appearance' means what? Are they two different things?

Student: My understanding is that it is by misreading these things that we create the duality between self and other. And when we really recognise self-clarity and clarity of appearance they are actually non-dual.

Rinpoche: That is how it is described. The example usually given is the one of the lamp. Say there is a lamp with a flame, and the flame is clear. Wherever there is a flame, there are its rays. It emits rays. Now, in the same way, because the nature of mind is awareness and is clear, it also has its radiance of clarity. There are different translations – 'clear' and 'clear appearance' is one thing you can call it.

This radiance of the clarity is the radiance of the mind. They are not two separate things. But what is this radiance? This radiance is the thoughts; this radiance is the emotions; this radiance is the perceptions; this radiance is the experiences, including anger, desire, pride and so on. All these things are actually radiance. In the Buddhist way of understanding, there is nothing actually wrong with the radiance at all. But when we don't understand the radiance, we develop a way of looking at it which becomes dualistic. Instead of thinking, 'This radiance that I see, or this clarity that I see, all around, is the reflection of my mind'; we say 'I am experiencing something and it is out there.' Then we start thinking, 'This experience, I like... This experience, I don't like...' And in that way we then create fears and attachments and the whole samsaric way of reacting arises.

The basis of this samsaric reaction is nothing other than 'clear light.' There is nothing wrong with it, only with our perception of it. If we could only understand that everything we experience is the self-illumination, the self-radiance, of our own basic awareness, it would not be necessary to be afraid of anything or attached to any experience.

When you understand this deeply then you will no longer run after things or run away – you will be liberated. You can self-liberate thoughts and emotions. And that is the whole point. Then whatever arises will not cause reactions like fear or attachment because everything is then wisdom.

The Causes of Maras and their Activities   73

When we talk about wisdom and mind poisons – they are the same thing; they come from the same radiance. If we are not aware of this, or if we do not understand it, it becomes the mind poisons. If we understand it well, then it is wisdom. There is nothing wrong with the way it arises, only the way we experience it can be wrong.

So what we have to do, firstly, is we need to familiarise ourselves deeply with what our consciousness is and what our awareness is. This means not just making our mind calm through *shiné* [calm-abiding] meditation and things like that. Making our mind calm is nice, but it is not liberating. Those meditations are very good because they make us calm and give us some freedom to manage our emotions. They are very good, but they are not liberating. However strong our meditation of this type may be, it will not make us enlightened.

The main thing we need to do is to understand, and familiarise ourselves deeply with, what our consciousness is and what our mind is. And particularly we need to do this, *not* through concepts. If what I have just described is treated only as concepts, as a philosophy, it will not help much. Instead, through meditation, we allow that experience of non-dual awareness to actually manifest, by learning how to be natural.

Of course shiné meditation and similar practices help us to learn to let our mind be completely natural. We need to learn how to not make any alterations, any 'It should be like this….It should not be like that…' When we can let it be in its natural state, we can bring out the natural qualities and experience them. This is then like Mahamudra and Dzogchen, and it is nothing to do with 'trying.' Our problem is that we are always 'trying' to do things, because that is our natural tendency. It is very difficult for us to *not* try. But that is what we need to do. Because the point is that there is actually nothing wrong with how our mind is in its original state. The only thing is that it has become so… Let us say I take a piece of paper and crumple it up into a tight ball. And then I try and turn it back into its original condition. It would take some time, no?

What would you call that?

Students: The mind is polluted?
The mind is crumpled?
Distorted?

Rinpoche: Distorted, yes. The mind has become distorted in its way of seeing, so that it is difficult to return it to its original state, its natural state.

Emotions when we are enlightened

Student: So, if someone is enlightened do they still have similar experiences, but they just don't 'interfere with' them? For example, if they saw something horrible, they would not experience it as 'horrible' but just as a radiance? Or do these things no longer exist for an enlightened person?

Rinpoche: I think it is like this– I think but I cannot know for certain as I am not enlightened. It will depend on how many habitual tendencies the person still has. When somebody has a high level of realisation then that person may still become angry, but they can release it immediately. It doesn't stick. It doesn't become hatred. Because the anger doesn't stick, they can liberate it. For example Marpa the Translator was a very angry person. Even after he became enlightened he was angry sometimes, and he used to go really mad, and turn red and blue, and take his stick and lash about! But immediately afterwards – nothing – it was completely gone.

Therefore, emotions will still arise in an enlightened person, but they will not be under the control of those emotions. Many scientists have observed His Holiness Dalai Lama closely for a long time and they say that his emotional reaction is the same as anybody else's would be. Sometimes it is even stronger – he cries, he can be angry. For example, he was once in a meeting or something like that, and someone told him that a child in Dharamsala had died. When he heard this, his face completely crumbled and he shed tears like any ordinary parent. He completely broke down. But two minutes later, he was laughing his heartiest laugh as if nothing had happened. They found the change of mood very interesting – that he could be completely sad one moment and completely happy the next.

I think that is exactly what happens. The emotions no longer bind you. That is why the emphasis in the teachings everywhere is on learning how to self-liberate thoughts and emotions, because this is the main way of liberating or freeing yourself. Usually we are bound by our emotions. Something happens and then the effect of it stays and we cannot get rid of it – it takes a long, long time. And that is even if we want to get rid of it! But maybe, when you are completely enlightened, maybe that no longer happens. I don't know!

Student: Children are very much like that. They can go from one emotion to the next and forget about it very, very quickly.

Rinpoche: Yes, that's true. The less you hang on to it, the less the mind holds onto something as too 'real' or too 'solid,' the easier it is to let go.

Student: So, is it a sign of progress to be hanging onto your emotions less and less?

Rinpoche: Yes, certainly. That is a really good sign.

Lust as a cause for maras

Student: You spoke about lust being a cause for maras. I was wondering if it was always a cause of maras or whether it is a specific type of lust that is the problem - because obviously lay people in a relationship will experience lust. I was wondering if you could elaborate?

Rinpoche: The text doesn't name any specific type of lust. Anyhow, do you think it is only lay people that know lust?

Marpa's anger

Student: If, when Marpa had a really bad fit of temper, he could let it all go because he was enlightened, he could then recover immediately. But what about the people around him, would they not still be feeling the effect of his bad temper?

Rinpoche: Very badly probably.

Student: So, should we not be careful about how we express our emotions?

Rinpoche: Yes, we should; we have to be very careful. I am sure Marpa's anger affected many people, and sometimes maybe in a bad way. But his wife, Dagmema, seemed to not be very much affected by it. She was a very fine lady. If the story is correct, one day when Dagmema came in, Marpa snapped his fingers, and she dissolved into light and then merged into his heart and then he passed away. Therefore, in a way, she was as realised as he was, and maybe even more so – although she never taught. The Tibetan women are like that.

78

The Six Remedies

Now we come to how to deal with these maras: how to pacify and get rid of them. Patrul Rinpoche recommends six methods or remedies.

1. Meditating on the Ultimate Nature: Emptiness

Generally the root cause of the maras is our self-clinging, our ego. Patrul Rinpoche quotes the *Bodhicharyavatara* by Shantideva, usually translated as the 'Way of the Bodhisattva':

'All the harm with which this world is rife,

All fear and suffering that there is,

Clinging to the 'I' has caused it!'

Way of the Bodhisattva, Ch. 8 'Meditation'

This is the strongest mara; the biggest evil and the most damaging spirit. All the sufferings in this world come from clinging to a self. The *Bodhicharyavatara* is saying we should feel like, 'I don't need that!' All maras arise in our own mind, so if your mind is clean, if your mind is purified, there can be no mara. The understanding is that when you notice the mara or obstacles, what you call 'obstacle' or 'mara', you can also notice it is all in your thoughts. What we call 'me', the 'obstacle' or 'mara', and 'obstructing', they are all concepts. It is all the play of your

The Six Remedies   79

own mind. So, in a way, they are 'unreal' in their very nature. They are like a mirage. There is nothing truly there. But the minute you grasp at it, and for as long as you do - whatever was your experience - then, the maras will be there, and they will affect you.

So, therefore, when you transcend this view, and your fear and attachment, all these obstacles and maras, kind of dissolve of their own accord. We can transcend these maras by learning to experience them with equanimity – equanimity in the understanding of emptiness.

If you understand that, then there is nothing called 'obstacle' or 'mara', because there is nothing that is separate from the interdependent nature of all things. It is all part of the Dharmata. The mara just arises, like your own shadow. There is no need to be afraid of it, and no need to be attached to it. If you can take the maras, any obstacle, without aversion or attachment but just completely in your stride - with that understanding, the mara will be transformed into the path. Then there is nothing called 'mara' to get rid of. There is also nothing to attain. Therefore, there is no duality.

Whenever you feel there is something like 'mara' coming, or a problematic situation arising, just let your mind relax in that. But for this approach to work, you need to have some stability of the understanding of shunyata or emptiness. Once you have that, there will be no more maras for you!

So that is one remedy. It is a very important remedy. It is the ultimate remedy. No obstacle, no mara – nothing – can affect or harm people who have that kind of experience or understanding. It is said in the Prajnaparamita Sutra (I am translating from the Tibetan here):

> *'If somebody is wise and understands transcendental wisdom, and has an experience of looking into that, that person becomes like a bird in the sky: nothing can obstruct them from going through. So, therefore, no maras can be of any obstruction to them.'*

80 *The Six Remedies*

Patrul Rinpoche says that if somebody is practising the Paramita of Wisdom they cannot be harmed by any maras, or by anyone or anything that is on the side of the maras, including poisons, the elements or any weapons. He means that when you have this wisdom, then anything that is an obstacle or a mara is transformed into the path, into wisdom, and there is no more mara.

In the Buddhist world, some people believe that when you find certain obstacles or maras, one way of dealing with them is to recite the Prajnaparamita Sutras. If you have actually realised Prajnaparamita, wisdom, then you don't need to recite the sutra. But if you don't have that realisation, just reciting these sutras is supposed to help keep the maras away.

Student: Which sutras are you talking about here?

Rinpoche: Prajnaparamita Sutras: the sutras on Wisdom. *Prajna* is Sanskrit for wisdom; the Tibetan word is *sherab*. There are many Prajnaparamita sutras: long Prajnaparamita sutras, shorter Prajnaparamita sutras and very short Prajnaparamita sutras. The 'Heart Sutra,' which is the most famous, is the shortest of this collection of sutras, the most concise.

If you have true understanding of Prajna, wisdom, then even if the whole world is against you, you have no fear. Having an experiential understanding of emptiness, can transform you in such a way that you lose all your fear, and all your clinging. And when you no longer cling to things or feel fear, no mara can harm you. The mara is no more!

That is the highest antidote - but it is not necessarily easy to achieve. It is not enough to simply say, 'Everything is emptiness!' Maybe that will help a little, but really what is needed is an experiential understanding of emptiness or wisdom: understanding the interdependent nature of all phenomena, the relative nature of things, and the relative-ness of the relative nature. With that awareness, you can let your mind completely relax; your mind can relax without fear. That is the key - *without fear*.

The Six Remedies 81

2. Generating Bodhicitta and Compassion

We can meditate on and develop Bodhicitta, loving kindness and compassion, to pacify the maras. This is a most important approach and something that may be more easily done than realising the nature of emptiness. Patrul Rinpoche says that, generally, if somebody meditates on loving-kindness and compassion constantly, and if they develop an experience of loving-kindness and compassion in themselves, this is the strongest way to ward off all negative obstacles or the maras that could attack you.

This has two aspects I think. Firstly, when you have loving-kindness and compassion in your heart, then the way you react with anybody, or anything happening, will be pleasant, basically caring and kindly. Secondly, if you are doing something good for other people, feeling and reacting in a positive way, they will be less likely to react to you in a negative way. If you are pleasing somebody, or doing something nice for other beings or the environment, then people's reaction is more likely to be more positive; most often it is like that. Usually how people react to you, how you find the people around you, very much depends on what kind of person you are – how you react, how you behave, how you present yourself, and how you communicate with those around you.

The more your mind is filled with loving-kindness and compassion, the more that loving-kindness and compassion is vibrated from your body, from your face, from your actions, from your words and the tone of your speech, from your smile. People like that. People don't like it when anyone gives off vibrations of anger or dislike or negative feelings.

For example, His Holiness the Dalai Lama, or His Holiness Karmapa, when people see them, they find they just like them. And they don't know why! Many, many times if His Holiness is giving a teaching, even on the highest philosophies of emptiness, when he talks for hours and hours on details that nobody understands, people still just sit there, smiling happily, happy to be in his presence.

Recently one of my cousins came from Tibet with his young wife. She had been educated by the Chinese – she was not really communist but communist-cadre – and she said to her husband, 'They say that people weep when they see the Dalai Lama. Now, the Dalai Lama is great but I don't understand why one should cry. I would never weep like that.' Then they went to Bodhgaya and saw the Dalai Lama. Later on, her husband teased her, telling us, 'She cried right from the beginning to the end!' It can be a bit like that – there is something that touches you, but you can't really describe it.

When people really embrace loving-kindness and compassion, then it simply radiates out from their presence. And not only from their presence but it can also even be felt in things they have used, in the place where they have sat or places they have been to – that is the basis of our calling certain things and places 'blessed' or 'holy.' There is so much positive vibrancy in such places, that people find all their negative feelings calm down. I once heard a scientist say he could not get angry for one year, after the Dalai Lama held his hand.

Another thing is that once you truly have loving-kindness and compassion, you don't really see the need to be angry or to feel hatred because you know very clearly that it is useless; it does not help anybody. You see it is not reasonable to get angry or have malicious thoughts towards anybody. Instead, you understand things, and even if harmful things happen to you, or if people do things to you that they should not do, even then your mind is calm. Your mind is full of compassion, so you find no need to hate. Just naturally, you don't react with violence or hatred. And when you don't react in this way, then there will be no more reactions from the other party, so things naturally calm down in you and slowly around you also.

When you have this inner calm, when you have this inner joy and contentment, there is no hate or chaos inside you. Then, whatever disaster happens cannot squash you; it cannot harm you because there

The Six Remedies

is no confusion inside. The more loving-kindness and compassion you have, the less you are vulnerable.

It is even said in the text here that, if you once help somebody or do something good for somebody, it is quite difficult to do anything bad against him or her after. Likewise, if you do something bad or harmful to somebody, it is naturally very difficult for him or her to do something good in return. This means that even if somebody does something negative to you, but you only react in a positive way in return, then after a while the whole situation naturally becomes less negative, and less aggressive – it cannot go on being negative all the time.

There are many quotations from the sutras saying that whatever maras, or obstacles, come to you, if your mind becomes absorbed in loving-kindness and compassion then this alone is enough to pacify them. When Buddha Shakyamuni meditated on great compassion, all the forces of mara that gathered to turn him off his path, with all their many weapons, were totally unsuccessful.

3. Through Devotion, Mantras and other Interdependent methods: Vajrayana Practices

Another way of pacifying the maras is through devotion, mantras and other Vajrayana practices, which work in an interdependent way. Patrul Rinpoche says that if you have a very clear devotion, to your Guru or your lineage or something like that, this will protect you from the affects of the maras. This means devotion with clear understanding and inspiration. Also, a very strong faith or devotion to the Buddha, Dharma and Sangha will protect you from being troubled by the maras.

'Taking Refuge,' for instance, is for this. Refuge is clearly mentioned in the text. Taking Refuge is not a prayer asking for help; it is making a decision, with clear understanding, about a sense of direction for yourself. It is a commitment. Going for Refuge to the Buddha is saying, from your heart, 'I want to be transformed. And I want all sentient beings to be transformed and towards that end I will work whatever may happen, and however long it may take, however difficult it may be.' It is a very sincere and very clear commitment to finding the right direction, the right purpose. 'And towards that end I would like to study and then use those understandings on myself, in order to work towards that goal.' That is then going for Refuge to the Dharma. 'In order to do that, I would like to try to find an environment for myself where there is a positive influence, not a negative influence.' That is the Sangha.

When you have these three commitments very clearly in your mind, the maras cannot affect you because you are so determined. Your direction is clear. Your mind is clear. And the more you remember that commitment and the more you think about it, the more your understanding of the Dharma will grow. Your view, your discipline and your devotion to your Guru will also all grow in this way.

The prayer 'Calling the Guru from Afar' is very important from the Vajrayana Buddhist point of view because, in the Vajrayana, remembering the Guru is remembering the Buddha, Dharma and Sangha. It is remembering the teachings and all the instructions; because all of this is embodied in the Guru. The Guru is nothing less than that. When you remember the Guru, you remember all these things. You associate with them again and so you remember your way or your path.

The more devotion you have to the Guru, the more your mind will be one with those qualities, those influences, that understanding. Consequently, when you have a strong, clear devotion to the Guru, your mind will cut off any negative influences. In a devotional state of mind there is no anger, no hatred, no sadness, no irritation, no sense of holding on to any kind of negative feelings. It is a pristine, clear, pure state of mind. There is a clear, positive non-conceptual emotion present, so it is not possible for any maras to affect you at that time.

Whenever there is a mara, or mara kind of obstacles, from the traditional Tibetan Buddhist point of view, calling the Lama and generating devotion is said to be the most important thing. You find this in traditional stories and also in many biographies, such as Milarepa's. Whenever anything negative comes, the instruction is to concentrate on devotion. And then you can say 'By the blessings of the Lama...' and all the negative forces, all the maras, are cleared. There have actually been many stories of things happening like that – people experiencing negative situations or being about to do something very negative themselves, and they stop because they remember their Guru.

This antidote also includes practising the mandala of your Yidam, if you have one. A Yidam is a practice like Chenrezig, Tara, Medicine Buddha or Vajrakilaya or many other deities, that a practitioner takes to be their main, or 'heart' practice. If you have such a practice and you can transform yourself – mind, body and speech – into the mandala of that deity, then through that you transform yourself into something totally pure. Every form, sound and state of mind has been transformed into the mandala of the deity: Form is the mandala of the deity; sound is the mandala transformed into wisdom. Therefore, there is nothing impure remaining, so there cannot be any maras.

Even if you cannot achieve this kind of high level of experience, doing a little bit of that kind of practice, such as saying the mantra of a deity, is still connecting yourself with this view. So it can bring a blessing and a protection and diminish your problems, maras and obstacles.

If you cannot access that kind of realisation through practice, or even see the possibility of it, then you can still use certain other methods at a more relative level. Realising the interdependent nature of all things, you can use things that are said to give protection, or blessing or things like special medicines. Nagarjuna, for example, prepared a mixture of different kinds of medicines to use or carry around with you. Or there are different types of yantras, or different mantras written down in certain ways, or reading sutras – all these things can also help to ward off negative influences and obstacles.

The main thing to understand is that, from the Buddhist point of view, everything is interdependent, sometimes in a seemingly insignificant way. Sometimes very small things can have an affect, if you know how to use them. In an ultimate way, everything is emptiness and there is nothing really truly existing. Now, because there is nothing truly existing, everything exists in a relative way, in an interdependent way. And in that interdependent arising of everything, there are so many causes and conditions that, if you know how to, you can do a really slight thing and it can have a big effect, in a positive or negative way.

So, therefore, if you are a skilful or a wise person, you can find ways to do even little things that will help a situation. This is like taking a little medicine or having a little acupuncture - you can sometimes get rid of the whole problem. Sometimes little things can ward off very big things, but if we are not aware of what is happening, we may not believe there is any connection. Sometimes it happens even if we don't believe it. But it is very important that we do not become too superstitious. So these are things we have to understand in a balanced way, and not become obsessed or neurotic.

I have heard that there was once a Westerner who went to a Tibetan Lama and learned how to do *mos*, which are a kind of divination, done with a mala. Then he started doing this divination for everything: 'Should I eat this thing today?' Yes? No? 'Should I go here?' Yes? No? And after some time he became so addicted to doing this, that he couldn't do anything without first doing a *mo*. His life became totally restricted by this; he was kind of frozen by it. He had to do a *mo* before every single action, and if the *mo* said 'Don't do it' then he wouldn't do it!

Life became very difficult for him, so he went back to the Lama and said, 'It's like this. I learned this divination from you, and I am so stuck with it now, so addicted, that I cannot do anything without a doing a *mo* first! Should I stop doing *mos*, or not?'

The Six Remedies 87

And the Lama said, 'Why don't you do a *mo* to see whether you should stop doing *mos* or not!' He followed this advice and did a *mo* to see whether he should stop doing the *mos*. And the divination said he should stop. So he stopped!

Sometimes too much is too much. Sometimes people depend on these kind of things too much and it becomes a problem.

4. Accumulating Merit and Positive Deeds

Here Patrul Rinpoche says that to read the profound sutras and tantras, or to write them down with your own hand is held to be a very good method for pacifying the maras. The following are also good things to do:

– *building stupas, large and small*
– *making different images of buddhas and bodhisattvas*
– *making tsa-tsas*
– *making offerings to the ordained sangha*
– *offering gifts and making contributions to people who are in difficult situations*
– *distributing food to children and to those who are sick or destitute*
– *making offerings to the spirits, like tormas*
– *performing fire pujas*
– *building roads – repairing the roads and clearing debris away.*

In Patrul Rinpoche's day people sometimes could not travel because of the poor condition of the roads, and it was regarded as a good act to put them right.

'Fire pujas' are also very positive and there are many different kinds. There is one kind called *sang*, where we make smoke offerings for purification, usually of a place. There is *sur* where we make an offering

88   *The Six Remedies*

of food and smells. Then there is *jinseg*, which is real fire, not just smoke (the Hindus also do this one as an offering), and many more.

All these positive things help subdue the maras by accumulating merit. The main understanding behind this is that whenever you do something very positive, your positive energy grows and therefore the negative subsides. This is how it helps deal with maras.

5. Developing Faith and Diligence

We discussed faith earlier, including inspiration, aspiration and certainty. This kind of faith and certainty means you become very clear and very certain about the path, the Dharma. However, you may have enemies or people who are trying to harm you, or even people near you like relatives and friends may try to harm you. Or you may have friends who lead you towards a wrong lifestyle. Or if you have a bad Lama, a bad teacher, who leads you into wrong practices, so your study, meditation and practice become negative. Or it may be that your mind poisons, or afflictive emotions, are too strong; or your grasping at the Eight Worldly Dharmas becomes too strong.

In all these cases, when any of these come or anything that we recognise as a mara happens, then at that time you should use your faith or certainty in the Dharma to re-inspire yourself. You should remind yourself of impermanence, of samsara, of Bodhicitta, and your mind will start to turn in the right direction again. You become inspired again and your mind becomes clear again - then nothing can harm you.

When your mind is clear and certain, and inspired in the right direction, you will naturally also become more diligent and find joy in doing positive things more easily. It is said, that if a person has faith and diligence, then no maras can waver him or her from the path. It puts it like this in one sutra:

'For example, if there is a big flowing river, it is impossible to make it flow upwards. In the same way, a bodhisattva who is intelligent and whose faith is stable and certain, or who has unwavering diligence, and a strong courage, no mara nor any kind of mara activity, can turn them from the path.'

Faith, diligence and clarity of the mind bring inspiration. And we should try to generate inspiration when we feel we are going a little bit off track, or having too many obstacles. We can do this by reading sutras or tantras that are inspiring; or reading or receiving inspiring teachings from great Lamas; reading or singing the songs of Milarepa or Patrul Rinpoche – these are all said to be inspiring for many people. Sometimes just listening to teachings on tapes or recordings may help. I have met many people who have said that sometimes they get fed up with the teachings, and they don't want to practice or meditate. Then sometimes they don't even want to listen to the teachings because they say, 'I've heard it all before!... There is nothing new.' Then sometimes, by chance, they come across a talk or a recording, and they start listening, and carry on listening, even though they didn't want to at first. And then something perhaps comes up that inspires them again, and at the end of the teaching, they find their attitude and their state of mind have completely changed.

So this kind of thing can also help. Sometimes we know things intellectually but it is easy to forget what really inspires us, what brings some kind of connection somewhere. We can say, 'Oh I know that already!' But our understanding hasn't gone deep enough to make a real connection, and then we are carried away by the mara.

6. Transforming your Mind or Attitude

Patrul Rinpoche says you can pacify, or transform the maras by changing your attitude, or the way you see things. This means transforming or changing your mind. Generally, he says, all maras and mara activities come out of one of the following:

our mind poisons

our doubts and strongly conceptual way of seeing things

our being too much affected by the Eight Worldly Dharmas.

Many examples are given, using different quotations from various sutras. For example:

'A practitioner who is on the path may have five maras to obstruct them on their way.

– *The mara of swirling concepts – like the way the clouds come, swirling or billowing*
– *The mara of laziness*
– *The mara of the distraction of wanting, like a desire for excess luxuries*
– *The mara of harsh speech, using harsh words which are like sharp weapons*
– *The mara of becoming angry and short tempered.'*

'When a Bodhisattva praises you and denounces others, you must understand that you are being affected by the maras.'

'The practitioner who does not want to sit alone and train their mind, which is most difficult to tame, but, instead, they go into public and try to teach Dharma in order to get wealth and fame– that is a sign of being distracted by the maras.'

The Six Remedies 91

'If you have a house and the house has certain holes, when winter comes the wind will come in wherever there is a little hole. So in the same way, the mara will find your weakness and insert itself. So you should guard your mind.'

The main understanding is that meditation, on emptiness and on the nature of the mind, offers over-all security, you could say. Otherwise, from time to time, you can try to look at your experience, your own mind, and see what is happening. And if there are negative emotions coming up, like hatred, too much greed or too much desire, arrogance, envy or jealousy, then you are holding on to your ego too much; too much self-clinging. Likewise, if you feel fear, unhappiness, doubts or have too many expectations, too many aversions, too many worries even, these are also a sign of clinging to your notion of 'self'.

So whenever something like that comes up you should try to work on it as soon as you notice it. First, try to relax in that experience. Use whatever instructions you have had: meditation instructions if possible, or if not, any means of relaxation you know, or at the very least, whatever instructions you have had on changing your attitude. Or you may try to allow a more positive side of your thoughts and emotions to come in, if you are able to. Or, if nothing else, at least learn not to react to those kinds of negative actions, emotions or thoughts, but just be in the present moment, and let things calm down. So whatever experience, or trainings or instructions you have – use them.

The understanding is that when something first comes up, a thought or emotion, if you are able to work on it at the very moment you become aware of it, you can then let go of it more easily. But if you allow it to build up and build up, it will become very large and strong, and thus be more and more difficult to handle. When the emotions become too strong they become like habits made of concrete, and will be much more problematic. So, therefore, try to catch them as quickly as possible and let them go.

Problems start with little things and if you can let go the moment you become aware of them, they won't harm you, they won't harm other people and you will be able to let them go without too much problem. But if you react when something comes up, and react with other people, they will react back, and the whole thing quickly escalates. After some time, even if you want to let go, it is too difficult. There are too many things involved and too many people involved; the situation has become too complicated and totally overwhelming.

So the understanding here is to become aware of these things when they are small and then it is easier to let go, it is easier to change, and easier to make it right.

It is important to allow ourselves to be just a little bit happy – we can enjoy whatever is good without needing all the time to be overly happy, without *needing to be happy* all the time. If we feel too strongly we must always be happy, and we should never be unhappy, that in itself becomes a problem. So, if I look at myself and see a very strong notion of 'I want to be happy!' Then that is the time to bring my mind home and say 'There is no need to be happy. It's okay.' and then you can calm down and understand that it is okay not to be happy and even okay to be unhappy. It is the same if you feel always, 'I need to be liked! I need to be loved! I need to be the star!' It is okay for it not to be just as you want it all the time.

When you see these problems coming up in your mind, you must catch them and must say to yourself, 'It's not like that!' Of course everyone wants to be happy. It is not wrong to be happy; it is good to be happy. But your happiness can actually be destroyed by 'wanting to be happy' – that 'wanting' brings unhappiness. If you 'want to make everybody happy', that brings unhappiness - because you can't make everybody happy.

The Six Remedies   93

Things like this have to be understood in context. So, whether it is understanding the Eight Worldly Dharmas or anything like that, then you have to bring the understanding deep into your heart and say, 'It's okay. It doesn't matter!' If you are too high, too happy, this brings the lows. So, if you find yourself too high, then you say to yourself, 'There is no need to be so excited about that.' Likewise, there is no need to be too unhappy or too down. You must find the balance. By understanding the nature of samsara, by understanding impermanence, by understanding the 'unreal' nature of things, their interdependence and dependent arising, by understanding all these things you can bring some kind of sanity to your mind. Try to bring sanity to your mind.

If you think, 'I am so great!' That kind of thing also brings you down, because you are not like that. Likewise, 'I am so bad!' Because you are not like that either. You need to find the balance and then you will have a little bit of peace of mind: a serene mind, a balanced mind. What would you call it, a 'balanced mind?'

Student: Composed?

Rinpoche: Yes, composed but also harmonious. Harmonious, balanced – not too much this, not too much that, but with a certain understanding and stability. Try to be a little bit aware, a little bit mindful, a little bit careful and not completely out of control.

It is said in the Düpa (Condensed Prajnaparamita) sutra,

> *'Whether you are walking or travelling, whether you are lying down, or sitting, whatever kind of actions or activities you are doing, be mindful of what is going on. Look around, but not too far; do not let your mind be totally deluded or distracted. Put on clean clothes...' Yes, that is said here! '...and let your mind be free from disturbance and distraction. Not having too many expectations and not looking forward to, or not running after too*

much gain. People like this can never be affected by the maras.'

It is said that in the Könchog Tsegpa (Ratnakuta / Jewel Mound) sutra,

> *'If you have four things, then you can tame your mind, and cannot be affected by the mara.* And what are these four? -
>
> *Do not envy the success or gains of other beings*
>
> *Do not speak divisive speech*
>
> *Try to cause or lead many people into positive ways or try to cause many people to become positive*
>
> *Meditate on loving-kindness and compassion*
>
> *If you have these four then you can never be affected by maras.'*

What all this is saying is work on your mind and try to change your attitude so whenever a mara state of mind comes, then you can work on it using whatever method you know. Sometimes it is not so much about how many methods you know, or how deep and profound the methods are, it is more about doing it. It is like the cat and the fox. You know the story about the cat and the fox?

A cat was sitting in the sun, on top of a fence or wall or something, and a fox came by. The fox looked at the cat and said, 'What are you doing there?'

'Oh, I am just resting!'

'Resting?! You are so lazy! You never do anything! If the dogs come chasing you, how many tricks do you know to get away from the dogs?'

'Oh, I don't know - I only know one!'

'Oh, you know only one! That's not enough! I know hundreds.'

Then they heard the dogs coming along. The cat quickly jumped up to the top branch of a tree and sat there. 'I'm here. This is enough. Now you show me how many tricks you have.' The fox ran here, and ran there,

The Six Remedies   95

and showed all his tricks. But in the end the dogs caught him.

So the cat had only one trick – but it worked. I don't know if this example really fits this situation or not, but what I am saying is that it is not about how many methods you know, the important thing is that you apply them. Even if I know all the methods, if I don't apply them, they won't work. If I know just one method, and I do it, then it might work.

Someone told me she was taught one method from the Zen tradition that, whenever something negative comes up, you bow down, to it. Then it will be okay in one way or another. It is a simple method but if it works, do it. It is like that. Even the very simple methods are okay. Sometimes, the simpler the better; if it means you apply them and use them. But even if you know hundreds of methods, if you don't apply any of them, they are all useless.

Final Questions and Answers

Yantras

Student: Rinpoche, you mentioned 'yantras'. Could you talk a little bit about them as this is not usually covered. The Samye Ling gate has a yantra on the underside of it. And I have come across them in the Bardo Thödrol texts, placed on the body. I notice a lot of the writing is in the *uchen* form of Tibetan; obviously this is significant in a Tibetan context but do you think this is equally significant in a land where that language isn't used?

Rinpoche: There are many things like that. Some come from India, some not. Those that do not come from India don't use Sanskrit. Some *dharanis*, or *bajra* in Tibetan (a type of ritual speech similar to a mantra) that the Buddha taught, are included in yantras. *Bajra* is like a banner, a 'banner on the top' mantra, like a Bodhisattva's white umbrella. They are often recommended to be recited or put on prayer flags or put on a flag on top of your house to bring positive things and get rid of maras and problems.

Then you also sometimes find them in *terma*, or 'treasure findings.' For example, there is a set of teachings called '*Lama Gongdü*' which was discovered by a *terton* ['treasure finder'] called Sangyé Lingpa. It comprises thirteen volumes and is one of the main Nyingma practices. It includes many teachings on the Dharma but it also has one section with predictions for the future. This text includes several yantras and also *khorlos* – ways of drawing various designs and mantras on a piece of paper. You then have to fold this paper in a certain way, tie it with colourful threads, in a certain way, and then bless it in a certain way. And it will give certain protections. There are things to increase your life, get rid of your diseases, to get rid of pests, to guard against fires in

The Six Remedies   97

your house, or to help if you don't sleep well – so many different things, around 108. I don't know whether they help or not. It looks like they do. I usually bring some with me when I travel and give them to people.

Before eating

Student: Before we eat our food we are supposed to offer it to the Three Jewels, I understand. At this point what should we visualise?

Rinpoche: The Buddhist way of looking at this is slightly different from the Christian. In the Christian approach they say, 'Thank you' before they eat, based on the understanding that the Creator has created the food. You are grateful for this, so you say 'Thank you!' Buddhists don't necessarily see it that way so they don't thank anybody, but they make it into an offering. The understanding is that whatever food you have, you offer it to the Buddhas, the Bodhisattvas, to all enlightened beings, out of gratitude as a kind of appreciation of them, before eating. You can be grateful for the food also. There is nothing wrong with being grateful! Eating is very important – you have to do it all the time to sustain yourself. So you can remember this too when you offer your food.

Usually you make it an offering to the Buddha, Dharma and Sangha and sometimes perhaps to Chenrezig and then finish the meal with a form of dedication. This is done in certain monasteries but not with too much ceremony. You take a little bit of food or something like that, put it to one side and then dedicate it. A bit like in the fire puja *sur*, but we don't burn it. We dedicate it to beings like the hungry ghosts and then put it outside – for the birds perhaps.

It is a way of connecting yourself with wisdom and compassion. Bodhicitta has two aspects, like two wings – wisdom and compassion. The wisdom is the Buddhas and Bodhisattvas and the object of the compassion is all sentient beings. So by doing this practice you are making an offering and a dedication, both to the wisdom beings and all sentient beings. You are not just diving into your food, but making it into a practice.

Student: If you are eating meat, do you still offer to the Three Jewels?

Rinpoche: Yes! You make an offering of whatever you are eating.

Vajrakilaya practice

Student: You mentioned Vajrakilaya practice, which is commonly used for overcoming obstacles. Is there any reason why that particular practice is more useful than, say, the normal Chenrezig practice for that purpose? Especially as ultimate compassion is quoted as the most potent force against the maras?

Rinpoche: Yes, that's true but then in Vajrayana Buddhism we have a variety of practices associated with certain energies, including certain Buddhas. For example, the Medicine Buddha is supposed to be more connected with healing. In the same way, Vajrakilaya is supposed to be effective for protection. There are a few others like that. There is Tara practice to ward off the outer fears and obstacles, and *Achala* to ward off the inner, especially practice-related, obstacles. Vajrakilaya is similar and held to be particularly effective for warding off obstacles, and creating the right atmosphere for positive activities. That doesn't mean that the other practices do not have those qualities – but that is how it is usually said.

Knowing one, knowing all

Student: You said, 'In knowing one, you know everything. Go to the root. The edges, the branches, don't matter.' Can you talk a bit about the branches?

Rinpoche: 'By knowing one, you know everything!' I think that what I was referring to was the nature of mind.

The Six Remedies   99

Student: I get the message about the root. But what are the branches?

Rinpoche: What was I saying about the branches?

Various Students: Relative reality? False appearances?

Rinpoche: Maybe I said something like, sometimes one has to go 'inwards.' Dharma understanding is to find the 'one', the nature of your mind. Then through knowing that, you know everything. By knowing one, you know everything. By solving one problem you solve all problems. And that is the opposite of what we usually do. Usually in academic study and research we go outwards.

I sometimes explain it like this. The Buddhist way of research and discovery is different from that used in science. If you want to know, to understand and fully discover something in Buddhism, the method is 'going inside.' By knowing one, you know everything.

The usual way in science or other studies is going outwards. You understand this branch, and then you understand that, and what is that element – one thing leads to another. You go more and more into the details; you understand the details of everything and your knowledge becomes very broad. The Buddhist approach is to go deeper, and so to go to the root. These are two approaches to knowledge, we could say?

Student: They talk about inductive and deductive knowledge?

Rinpoche: Could be that.

What really works?

Student: Could you say something about what you have found is most useful in all the teachings? And whether that has changed over the years; whether you have applied different methods for different times; and what has been the most practical?

Rinpoche: I only know that if you don't apply it, it doesn't work! I really don't consider myself a great example of practice. I don't know what works. Usually I find the right attitude very important. I am not sure whether I have overcome much negativity or really transformed my mind through meditation, because I don't meditate too much – that's why I call myself 'Lazy Lama!'[1] I know it is good to meditate, and I almost know how to meditate – but still I do not meditate! So I must be lazy, there is no other reason.

I think if you meditated, it would be really useful. But I cannot tell you how much, because I don't do it. But I think attitude really helps a lot because the right attitude can change your way of reacting to things and then you can really let go.

I don't know if I have told you this story? When I was very young, I had a reputation of being a very angry, quarrelsome boy, aggressive and attacking anybody. I was also, I think, a little bit caught up in a cultural attitude. Tibetans – not all Tibetans – but the Khampas give a lot of importance to bravery, especially in boys. If you are not brave, you are nobody! You can be intelligent, you can be well-behaved, you can be anything but it doesn't matter at all unless you are brave. All boys have to be brave and everything is done to make them so. Mixed in with the first meat they ever eat as babies, is a bit of wild yak's heart so they become like a wild yak. I am supposed to have had it, but it doesn't seem to have affected me!

So I was acting brave, I threw stones at people and fought everybody, even big boys. When I was fighting I used to go really red, beat with my fists, kicked; I even butted with my head - everything. Then at a

The Six Remedies   101

certain point I changed. And I think I changed after I had studied the *Bodhicharyavatara*, when I was around 10 or 11 years old.

I think your attitude, the way you see things is very important. I really think that a change of attitude can change your whole way of being, your reactions – because most of our reactions are formed by our attitude – 'it has to be like this... It can't be like that' and so on.

Previously, when somebody said something against me, I would fight them; even if I couldn't beat them, I would still fight them. Later on, I wouldn't fight. I would say, 'It doesn't matter. If they want to say bad things, what does it matter? It is their waste of energy.' So, I didn't react – and then it *didn't* matter. In the end, I was the winner. And if what they accused me of was correct – especially if I was like that - then they were right, so what could I say? It's okay. And if it is not okay, if it is not right, then I should change. If what they say is wrong, then sooner or later it will come out. So there is no need to be too angry about it, because if you are angry, that achieves nothing. Therefore, it is still okay even if what they say is wrong. In the long run I have to do what is good for me. It doesn't matter what people say, that is not the issue. The issue is to do something that is good for me, and maybe good for others.

So if I consider the best way to make progress, it is rarely useful to become too involved with little things. Little things don't matter much and the involvement gets you nowhere. The main thing is to be clear. So I think it is very important to have the right attitude.

It is also important to have some awareness of what is going on: awareness of what you are doing with your body, speech and mind. It is extremely important to be aware of this because most of the time we are looking outwards. We are not looking in; we are not looking at ourselves. If we have a problem with somebody else, our tendency is to blame that person. But if I look carefully, then I can see why he said this, why he did that and if I see this, then my attitude changes. And when I change, it changes my reaction. Most of my problems actually come from

102   *The Six Remedies*

me, which is why I think it is very important to be able to look clearly at yourself. All these mind poisons – they are there and I don't think we can uproot them very easily. To uproot the mind poisons is not easy, but managing the mind poisons is not so difficult. We need to manage our mind poisons and not let them grow out of proportion or out of control, because otherwise they create problems for self and problems for others.

So my practice is extremely simple; it is not very complicated and not very high! I know high practices also, very profound practices, and if I did them, I think they would work. Yes, I think they would work and I shall do them sometime in the future... after I have retired.

Maras and habits

Student: Can a mara become a habit? Could you end up being caught in it so the mara just repeats itself?

Rinpoche: Exactly! That is very common.

Student: And how do you counter that because, presumably if it has become a habit, it is even more difficult.

Rinpoche: It is much more difficult and most of our maras have actually become firm habits already.

Mahamudra

Student: It is a huge subject, but could you say a bit about Mahamudra?

Rinpoche: I can say something very short about Mahamudra. Tibetan Buddhism follows what is known as the 'Nalanda University tradition.' All Tibetan Buddhist schools follow this tradition. Nalanda was a big Buddhist university in India and all the key people were there at some point: Nagarjuna and Naropa and Atisha Dipankar and Shantideva and many others, were all from there. Guru Padmasambhava, too, spent some time there. And this tradition has, as its basis, the Vinaya, or basic conduct. Then it has the practice of the Bodhisattva, which is the main practice, the Six Paramitas. And then on top of these there are the Vajrayana practices, which were not practised openly but more secretly. This is the general approach.

Mahamudra is the quintessence of all of these. It is like the pith of all the tantras, including the highest tantras; and not only the tantras, but the quintessence of the whole of Buddhist understanding. If a great master of this whole experience should put together the essence, the heart, of all those things, and present it to his student – not as an elaborate teaching but as a direct instruction; a great master, somebody who has studied many, many years, has practised many, many years, has taught the sutras and tantras and all sorts of practices, and at the end says from his or her experience, 'Of all that can be studied and practised - the real essence is Mahamudra.' It is like that. It is the quintessence, the experiential quintessence, of the whole of the tantras.

That is then taken and given as an instruction, which can be very short. It comes direct from the Lamas, as a kind of lineage or special practice, and is more of an experiential instruction. It was not written down at all for a long time. It includes everything within it, including the highest and deepest instructions, from beginning to end. These are called 'pith instructions' because they are the essence. Once you have some experience of this, you understand the whole of the sutras and tantras. Whereas, if you study sutras and tantras, then you have knowledge within them, but it is not so easy to understand the essence. This is what makes Mahamudra extremely important.

'Mahamudra' is this kind of teaching in the Kagyu lineage. The equivalent teaching in the Nyingma lineage is called 'Dzogchen.' In the Sakya lineage it is called 'Lamdré' and the Gelugpas sometimes use Mahamudra coming from the Kagyus. The traditional approach in Mahamudra is that you first start with *Ngöndro*, ('*Ngöndro*' means preliminaries). When you have finished the Ngöndro, you then progress to shamatha, then to the vipassana, and finally to Mahamudra. This is one traditional way of doing it, but you do not have to practise Ngondro before shamatha and vipassana practice.

Mahamudra itself has nothing to do with any culture. It is completely free of culture. But the Ngöndro was designed, of course, for Tibetans, and it has something of a Tibetan cultural aspect to it. If you understand it clearly, anyone from any culture can connect with these practices. But I find that sometimes people in the West do not connect so well with it because of that cultural aspect, because they do not understand what it is about. So the Ngöndro part may only be a useful practice if you can really connect with it, through understanding it. But Mahamudra crosses all cultures.

Visiting different cultures

Student: You were talking about cultivating a balanced, harmonious mind – you said that too high can lead to too low, and so on. And it seems to me most of what we have been talking about is abolishing extremes. But in some contexts I wonder if extremes may be quite wholesome. For example, I went to India earlier this year and had very intense experiences and came back 'flying,' from it all, going to holy places and meeting holy people. But I don't know how to balance that sort of thing at all?

Rinpoche: Maybe if you went there several times it would help! That is what I am talking about: a little bit of something like that is not too bad. It is something that often happens to people if they go somewhere really different, not just to those who are Dharma practitioners. For many people from the West, going to India is a shock! I know many people who went to India, planning to stay there a few months, got as far as Delhi or Calcutta and came back. When you first go there it can be a real shock!

The Six Remedies   105

And then when you come back – it is another shock! Sometimes even worse. At first I didn't understand that. I understood the shock of going there, but the shock of coming back, I didn't understand at all – probably because I never experienced any shock myself. I never got a shock either coming here or going there. I was never 'flying' at all at any time! - Too thick, probably.

When I first came to Europe, however, I found this whole idea of privacy very strange. Always: 'Please excuse me... excuse me... excuse me...' Even when somebody came in with some tea and biscuits: 'Oh excuse me, excuse me.' As if they were going to beat me up or something. It was a little too much. Even if somebody speaks to me, 'Oh I am taking your time... I am wasting your time...' as if I had something more important to do! Especially as I had nothing to do. People do things in different ways, of course, but coming to the West was never really shocking.

India was more of a shock for me. When I first came to India from Tibet it was really like coming from the 8th century into the 20th century. In Tibet there was nothing modern like trains, or cars, or aeroplanes. There were no banks where we lived, no shops. No one used cash and I had only seen a watch, my uncle had a watch. When we were travelling to India, someone told me, 'Today or tomorrow we will get to the border and then we will go by train. You will see a train.'

So I asked, 'What is a train?' I had never seen a train.

'A train is something made of iron. The whole body is made of iron. It rolls... on a road of iron. And you can sit in it and you can put your cup of tea on the table and it doesn't spill!'

So I thought, and thought, about what this train could really be like. It rolls, so I thought it must be a ball - I hadn't really seen any wheeled vehicles. We didn't even have bullock carts in my part of Tibet, as it is too mountainous; no bullock carts, no horse carts, nothing like that. So, I thought, a train must be a big iron ball. And there must be a big flat iron road for this ball to roll along. But then how could somebody sit

106   *The Six Remedies*

inside? So then maybe, I thought, there are two balls – one outer ball and one inner ball. The people can sit in the inner ball; and the outer ball rolls, while the inner ball stays still, so people can sit in it and have a cup of tea. That is what I thought! My idea of the train was this kind of 'double-ball.'

Student: How old were you then?

Rinpoche: I was born in 1952 and this was 1959, so I was about seven years old.

Chöd practice: Cutting through

Student: Could you say a bit more about Chöd?

Rinpoche: Chöd practice: 'Cutting through.' Chöd is a traditional practice started by Machig Labdrön, a great female master in Tibet. She formed the Chöd practice herself, after having received teachings directly from an Indian master called Padampa Sangyé in Tibet, and from Kamalashila in India. You have heard of Kamalashila? He was a great master, a student of Shantarakshita who brought Buddhism to Tibet for the first time. Kamalashila came to Tibet and debated for two years with the Chinese Mahayana Master, Hashang. Kamalashila finally won and that is why Tibet follows the Indian lineage from Nalanda rather than the Chinese lineage.

The legend is that Kamalashila was a master of the practice of 'changing your body' – the ability to transfer your mind into another body - and then just get up and go in the new body! So one time when Kamalashila was returning to India from Tibet, he was walking through the Himalayas where there was not much of a road and he found a big elephant, dead on the track. He thought he would get rid of this because it was completely blocking the way. So he directed his mind into the elephant's body and 'walked' the body away. But when he returned, his

The Six Remedies   107

own body had gone! Padampa Sangyé who also knew how to do this practice had come along and seen Kamalashila's beautiful body just lying there. So he thought 'Oh this is such a nice body!' and 'went in' leaving his own ugly body behind. So Kamalashila was left with Padampa Sangyé's ugly body and he had no choice but to get into it.

Later on Padampa Sangyé came to Tibet three times and on one of these occasions he met a young Tibetan girl called Machig Labdrön. She was a special girl because she had a very great skill in fast reading. She read the Prajnaparamita Sutras so fast that she could read the whole twelve volumes in two or three days. Tibetans believe that if you read the Prajnaparamita Sutras, or someone reads them to you, all the maras will go away. So everybody invited Machig to read these sutras. And because she had read them so many times she gained a clear understanding of them. When she met this Padampa Sangyé for the first time, he only needed to give her one instruction and she got the whole deeper meaning. This instruction on the Prajnaparamita Sutras was given as a main, pith instruction. And later she formed this school of practice called 'Chöd'.

Chöd means 'cutting through'. And the Chöd tradition which she started became very popular in Tibet and was taken up by all schools: the Kagyus do Chöd, the Nyingmas do Chöd, the Sakyas and the Gelugs – everybody does Machig Labdrön's Chöd practice. There are many teachings on it in all these four main schools of Tibetan Buddhism.

Chöd practice is usually done with a drum called a damaru, a bell and sometimes a thigh-bone trumpet [a trumpet made out of a human thigh bone]. It is totally based on the understanding of Prajnaparamita and is to cut through the maras and get rid of them. Machig Labdrön herself was a wild yogini, roaming around and doing her practices. She put her son in a walled-in retreat for about twelve years or something. She was pretty wild!

Student: What are you cutting through in the practice?

Rinpoche: All the maras but mainly the ignorance of self-clinging. Cutting through ignorance is the main thing. The practice is to get rid of all your attachment, all your aversion and your fears. So, not in the beginning but after some time, people do Chöd practice in cemeteries or haunted places where they are more likely to feel fear. By doing Chöd you learn to face your fears and cut through them. There are sections in the practice where you visualise 'giving your body' to the spirits and things like that. It is to work with and totally eradicate our fear.

Student: Is this practice designed for both men and women to do?

Rinpoche: Yes. There is nothing in Tibetan Buddhism that cannot be done by both men and women.

110

Conclusion

Patrul Rinpoche concludes by saying the most important thing about maras is that you recognise them for what they are, and understand the best way to work on them. There are no maras, there are no obstacles, which cannot be pacified or turned around. They exist because of our way of reacting so, from that point of view, every mara can also be used as a kind of stepping-stone.

The challenge is to use the maras as stepping-stones, as fuel that can drive you forwards. If you don't have obstacles, if you don't have maras, you have nothing to work on. We can understand it like this: if we can cross this threshold and get through this mara, then we shall have reached another stage of practice. That is why a mara is not regarded as something negative, not in our practice generally and especially not in Chöd practice. There is always this view that in order to have understanding, you must first experience the power of the maras. The mara needs to be displayed before we can work on it. When that happens, if you are able to overcome it, you will have more confidence.

Confidence in your practice or stability in your practice can only be tested by something that comes as an obstacle, so obstacles have a role. It is a little bit like when you finish a course of study; in order to get the qualification, you have to first sit an exam. Only if you pass the test, will you get the degree. In that way the mara can almost become a support on your path, if you know how to deal with it. If you don't know how to deal with it, it becomes an obstacle. But if you know how to deal with it, then it becomes a support. It becomes something that increases your diligence. When an obstacle or mara appears you think, 'Aha! This is a mara, now I have to watch out. I have to work on this.' And working on it makes you more diligent and helps you feel more joyful in working on it.

It will bring more confidence and more certainty to your experience. It is also something that brings a connection: it connects you to the results and brings you towards accomplishments. The more you can overcome the maras, the nearer you are to realisation, thus maras are something that connect you to enlightenment. Mara activity can advance your practice – that is why it is sometimes said that the mara is an emanation of Buddha: it is Buddha activity.

Mara activity is something that is necessary or useful; it is not totally negative. This is why it is said that whether you become enlightened or not, depends on whether you can cross through the maras or not. The more maras you overcome, the more enhanced your practice will be. Once we understand it and work on it, a mara is not actually an obstacle. It is not an obstruction or something negative. So, it is very important that we know how to transform these maras into something useful and helpful.

A person who has faith, devotion and diligence, whatever outer, inner or secret maras arise, cannot really be obstructed by them. They cannot really be affected by the maras, or sink under their influence. I think it is important to understand, when we talk about faith or devotion here, the Tibetan word used is *depa*. 'Faith' is not really the right translation for *depa* but there is no other word in English so we have to use it. *Depa* is understood in three ways; and these three ways I translate as *inspiration*, *aspiration* and *certainty*. All three are *depa* and all three have a very strong sense of understanding and deeply feeling the truth - the way it is.

This is very important in Buddhism because Buddhism is completely based on understanding, on deep understanding and different levels of understanding. In Buddhism the basic idea is that human beings have the capacity to understand everything, and the capacity to understand things completely and clearly.

This faith is not that somebody gives you an order or a command, and then you have to do that: 'I must obey any command because I say I have faith.' That is not the idea, which is very different from many other religions. Sometimes you may hear these kinds of teachings – that you must have faith, and you must have devotion - and people assume that Buddhism is like any other religion where you have to listen to the teacher or whoever and they will tell you what is the right thing to do. You ask, 'What is right? What should I do?' and you are told, 'Do this. Believe this.' - 'Okay, I believe it!' That is not the approach in Buddhism; that is not the correct understanding. From the Buddhist point of view, *depa* is your own understanding, your own confidence, your own inspiration.

Of course people can give you guidance. People can teach you. We have to learn, but unless we do learn, there is no point! If they just tell you, 'Do this, and don't do that!' and you follow those orders without knowing why, it doesn't lead you anywhere. That is the Buddhist view, which is why studying is so important in Buddhism. 'Studying' means really finding out for yourself, learning, and thereby deepening your understanding; using your own wisdom and certainty to develop your own practice, knowing what is the right thing to do yourself.

When you have that understanding and confidence it should come together with what your teacher has said and what the Buddha taught, and you will develop yet more confidence. Then your enthusiasm, your certainty and your clarity will become stronger; your diligence will become clearer, enabling you to work on it. It is all about realising deeply that you have the capacity to know what is good, what is right, and what is not. That is the basic principle, the basic philosophy, that people have the capacity to know what is right and what is true.

If that understanding is not the foundation, then nothing else will work. So therefore that background understanding is crucial, because everything is taught on that assumption – that people have the capacity to know, to deeply understand what is right and what is wrong and what

Conclusion 113

is true and what is not true. So it follows that when you have faith it means your understanding is clear and that you have a kind of certainty. And because of that clarity your motivation becomes stronger.

To gain that kind of understanding you must have the right guidance and a 'genuine' Lama or teacher. They will give you clear instructions. And then you must also find some courage. We all need some courage and daring to improve ourselves, because to transform ourselves – that is an unknown experience. Realisation is an unknown experience. Anything that is not a habit of ours is an unknown experience. To break through our habits, our partialities and prejudices, brings us into completely unknown territory. And you cannot do that without some kind of courage and a little bit of self-confidence.

When we reach this kind of understanding, then whatever maras come can be seen as a *chag-deb*. *Chag-deb* means that it becomes like a horse whip that makes you go forward more quickly – especially if you understand things and have a good intelligence. If you study and acquire some sound knowledge all this becomes a support; and all the obstacles put forward by the maras become a support to your practice. When you understand the nature of ultimate reality, and you understand what the nature of your mind is, then, to that good practitioner, whatever happens is just a reminder or something that brings more realisation. Nothing is an obstacle anymore.

When that kind of understanding is there, whatever negative forces happen become like an ornament to the practitioner's mind. Here, 'ornament' means something that is helpful, something you place carefully to heighten and bring out the natural beauty. The word 'ornament' used like this, occurs in many Buddhist expressions and titles of teachings.

Patrul Rinpoche says that those people who do not have an authentic Lama or teacher, who don't have a connection with one, who haven't done much studying or received the right kind of instructions, and also those who have come under the power of very negative karmic influences – even if they have great faith or devotion and diligence – these people can be carried away by the maras.

The text says that even with diligence and devotion, until you have stabilised your mind, and achieved some stability in your practice, you should try to rely on the guidance of authentic teachers and try to get as many clear instructions as possible from different sources. It is especially important to have the key instructions on how to examine the maras.

The next part of the text emphasises the same thing. If you understand that all phenomena are emptiness; and you never withdraw your compassion towards other sentient beings; and you are very determined that whatever you have done you will not waver from the path; and you have devotion and a clear understanding of the Lama and the Three Jewels – Buddha, Dharma and Sangha – whoever has these four things will always attain victory over the maras.

In the absolute nature, there is nothing called 'mara', nothing with this name. Mara is not there on the absolute level. Maras are in the relative understanding; they arise in a relative way, from our own deluded minds. They come because of our delusions and are projections from our deluded mind.

Our deluded mind is the source of the maras. To those yogis who have an understanding or realisation of the ultimate nature, to them these relative obstacles are more like friends. There is nothing negative about them. They are something like an instrument or a stepping stone, or like something you play with. - 'Yogi' here means a practitioner, man or woman, who is totally committed to the Dharma. 'Yogi' does not mean only male yogis!

All these maras and obstacles and obscurations are objects of the view for these yogis. If the maras are not there, there is no object or view. Maras and obscurations are their objects of meditation. If there are no maras, there is nothing to meditate on. Maras and obstacles are their objects of practice – if they are not there, there is nothing to practice.

Conclusion 115

The maras are used as things that instigate or inspire the mind and if there are no maras, there is nothing to inspire the yogis, or us, to practice.

The maras and obstacles are the means whereby one can improve, and go beyond whatever level one is at. And if they are not there, there is nothing to give that push, that incentive. The obstacles are the *bridges*. There is an obstacle, you overcome that obstacle and that is an accomplishment. Accomplishment in what? That you can overcome an obstacle! That way you find that whatever obstacles come, you will have no problem with them. And they are the bridge to accomplishment.

The text even says here that suffering is the path to happiness! Because you understand that suffering is there and because you don't want that suffering, it makes you do something about it – it is a catalyst. So it makes the path. It is a catalyst for happiness because if you just kind of tolerate that problem - 'Oh, it is okay!' - nothing happens. But if it is not okay, then you do something about it.

If there is no problem, then there is no solution. The mind poisons, the kleshas, have the same nature as the wisdoms. So when there are no kleshas, there is no wisdom. The kleshas are the wisdoms that are not expressed well; they are 'unskilfully expressed wisdom.' Concepts and thoughts are the mirror of the natural Dharmata, the enlightened state. So when there are no concepts the Buddha-nature, the Buddha's enlightened mind, is the reflection of the conceptual mind.

Therefore, for the yogi who has the right understanding, an intelligent and clear understanding, there is nothing that is not good, everything is positive. Whatever untoward or unfortunate incidents happen – they are positive, they are good. This is why it is said – and I have said this many, many times – that the purpose of meditation is not about having a good experience, a pleasant experience.

If you meditate and then have a nice experience, it is all peaceful, it is all joyful. 'Oh! It is so nice!' That's okay in a way, but that's not the main purpose. Because when you have that kind of experience you say,

'Oh this is so nice; I hope this will not end!' Or you hope that something unpleasant will not come. And the moment you wish that – then it has ended! Because when you wish for something, you become fearful. The fear arises, 'Oh I don't want anything else, I want only this!' And when the fear comes, you are no longer peaceful. A fearful state of mind is not peaceful. So as soon as one comes, the other goes. Then you think, 'Oh I want that feeling back again!' And again, it is not possible because wanting something is not peaceful; wanting something is like holding something very hot and saying, 'I don't want to be burnt!'

The real result of meditation practice is not just having a good experience but that whatever experiences you have, you can deal with them. If you have a nice experience – you say 'This is very nice; it is okay! No problem. It can come, no problem; even if it goes – no problem, because it doesn't matter.' And if you have a less pleasant experience, such as some sadness, some disturbing emotions, maybe a few problems – even then you should say to yourself, 'It is not a nice experience but it is perfectly okay.'

When somebody can take good and bad experiences almost at the same level, and can deal with any experience without a problem – that is really what realisation is. That is the result of real meditation because then you have good experiences all the time. If a good experience comes, it is very nice; a bad experience comes and it doesn't matter so it is okay too. So then there are no bad experiences. So what is 'bad'? There is nothing 'bad' because there is nothing there.

So, if there is nothing 'good' and nothing 'bad' then everything is okay! When that experience comes really deeply, what we are talking about is the fourth Immeasurable Contemplation [*Brahmavihara* Sanskrit]: 'May all beings abide in great impartiality, free from attachment and aversion.'

This does not mean having no reactions or senses – a dull neutrality. It means being able to deal with anything, the good, and the not so good experiences like fear. Usually aversion is fear: 'I don't want it!' And then attachment is something that you do want. We need to get rid of the 'Oh this is very bad, I can't take it!' Or 'This is very good; I must keep hold of it!'

Of course, everybody wants to keep what is good and avoid what is bad. But it is better to learn deeply how to experience things in such a way that 'bad' doesn't become too heavy and 'good' also doesn't become a problem. That is 'wisdom'. 'Wisdom' is knowing how to transform things so they do not feel so heavy; and how to let them come and go, understanding that whatever arises in your experience is just an experience arising, and it will come – and it will go. It is not necessary to run away from it and neither is it necessary to run after it. If you do run away, there is nothing to run away from; it is just your own experience. So, instead, you can try to enjoy it, in a way. If you can see it as a display of your own mind, you won't be so troubled by it.

When you achieve that, when any kind of a mara experience comes, there is no negative force to it. It has no negative power. The word 'negative' means something that we don't want, something that is bad; 'I don't want it; I shouldn't have it'. So once you know how to deal with anything, then nothing is negative. You have overcome the maras, because if there is nothing negative, then there are no maras.

The maras are conquered. You have driven them away, to the other side of the ocean! This is a traditional image, or visualisation: you say mantras and, by this power, all the maras and all the negative things are driven out of this room, out of this country, out of this continent, to the other side of the ocean.

So, this whole teaching has come from a collection of teachings by Patrul Rinpoche. It originally comes from the Kadampa tradition, I think, and then it was a little bit abbreviated and presented in this way. We have not gone through it completely word by word, but we have more or less gone through the whole teaching. The only thing we omitted here were some special maras for very high practitioners!

119

120

Dedication

All my babbling,
In the name of Dharma
Has been set down faithfully
By my dear students of pure vision.

I pray that at least a fraction of the wisdom
Of those enlightened teachers
Who tirelessly trained me
Shines through this mass of incoherence.

May the sincere efforts of all those
Who have worked tirelessly
Result in spreading the true meaning of Dharma
To all who are inspired to know.

May this help dispel the darkness of ignorance
In the minds of all living beings
And lead them to complete realisation
Free from all fear.

Ringu Tulku

A Short Biography of Patrul Rinpoche

Patrul Rinpoche was a Tibetan Lama from the nineteenth century. He passed away in 1887, having lived about eighty years. So he was alive from around the beginning, to almost the end, of the 19th Century. He was recognised as a Tulku when he was very young -the reincarnated Lama of a monastery called Palge Monastery, in Eastern Tibet. After he had been educated there, though, he did not want to stay on at the monastery. He did not want to act like a high Lama. So, he abandoned his monastery and went away.

He went to study in a Dzogchen Monastery, under various different teachers, and received many profound teachings. His root guru was Jigme Gyalwa Nyugu, who was one of the main students of Jigme Lingpa. Jigme Lingpa was a great master of the Longchen Nyingthik, the main Nyingma teachings on Dzogchen, and was one of the two foremost holders of this Dzogchen lineage, together with Longchenpa.

Patrul Rinpoche became a very, very great scholar. He was considered to be one of the most learned people in Tibet at that time. Jamyang Khyentse the Great and Jamgön Kongtrul the Great were also very famous throughout Tibet. Together, they went on to found Rimé, an ecumenical, or non-sectarian, movement within Tibetan Buddhism. These two, and especially Jamyang Khyentse, became teacher to nearly all, high and low, learned and unlearned Lamas, especially in Kham; not only in the Kagyu or Nyingma or Sakya schools, but for all the schools of Buddhism in Tibet.

Once Jamyang Khyentse was asked, 'At this point in history we have these three great masters here: yourself, Jamgön Kongtrul and Patrul Rinpoche. You are all so great, but who is the greatest?' And Jamyang Khyentse said, 'As far as scholarship and learning is concerned, there is no debate; Patrul Rinpoche is the best. He is the highest, the most learned, person of all. There is no doubt about it.' Then he said, 'As far as being able to benefit other beings is concerned, Jamgön Kongtrul is the greatest. There is no doubt about it. His works are so important and he benefits so many people as well as the teachings.' Thirdly he said, 'As far as realization is concerned, then maybe I am also not so bad.'

So Patrul Rinpoche has always been regarded as a most learned person. One particular story that shows what he was like is about a sectarian group in Tibet at his time, who were very fundamentalist. They used to ask travellers which sect they belonged to and only let them pass if they said they belonged to their own sect. Patrul Rinpoche came travelling by that way and they asked him which school of Buddhism he followed.

He said, 'I don't know. I just follow Buddha's teachings.'

They couldn't identify any sect from that, so they thought they would ask which Yidam he practised.

He replied, 'Oh, I practise Bodhicitta.'

Bodhicitta is something very universal, nothing very specific, but it is the main practice. So they still couldn't find out! Whatever questions they asked, he answered in such a way they could not identify any particular sect.

Patrul Rinpoche used to call himself 'Tattered Old Dog', a name given him by his Guru. Somebody once sent me a photo that was said to be of Patrul Rinpoche. I don't know whether it is really of him, but such a photo does exist. He did not wear monastic robes, choosing instead to wear the clothes of an ordinary person - a woollen sheepskin and so on. He would travel, not telling anybody who he was; just appearing very, very ordinary. So he managed to travel all over the place without anybody knowing who he was or exactly where he went.

In spite of this, he did give many teachings, sometimes secretly. Some of the most important Dzogchen and Mahamudra lineage teachings – very special lineages that are still kept alive today – have come from Patrul Rinpoche. His disciples included many masters of the Sakya, Gelugpa, Kagyu and Nyingma schools. He spent most of his life in retreat in remote places most people could not even stand. He went to the North-Eastern part of Tibet, for example, where only wild yaks and wolves lived. There would be nobody else there, except sometimes bandits would come. Patrul Rinpoche would stay there, in retreat, carving stones, carving the mantra *Om mani peme hung* into them. He made a big, big 'mani wall' from these stones in a place where nobody ever goes.

Only really determined, single-minded people could go to Patrul Rinpoche and - sometimes - get teachings. He would usually say, 'Why do you come here, to this godforsaken place? There are such great teachers, in Derge and other places, like Jamyang Khyentse and Jamgön Kongtrul and many other masters. There are so many institutions and monasteries. But, abandoning them all, you come here to see this old person who knows nothing! You are completely mad! You are totally deluded! I don't want you to waste your life. Go away! If you come near me, I will hit you with a stone!'

Sometimes he would even throw stones too. So it was not easy to get teachings from him, especially the deeper kinds. Sometimes people had to use tricks to get teachings from him because this was how he was.

There is a story about how a distinguished Lama from Palpung once persuaded Patrul Rinpoche to teach on the Bodhicharyavatara, 'The Bodhisattva's Way of Life'. The Lama had great devotion to Patrul Rinpoche and one day he announced, 'I will go and receive some Bodhicharyavatara teachings from Patrul Rinpoche.'

People said, 'You will not receive them. He is not the kind of person who teaches.'

But he said, 'Yes, I will. I know how to persuade him. I will go.'

So he went with his retinue to the place where Patrul Rinpoche was staying, under a rock in the wilderness somewhere, nothing special there at all, and they camped a short distance away. He pretended he didn't even know who Patrul Rinpoche was.

So... he camped. And then, after a while, he sent a little *tsampa* [ground roasted barley, a staple Tibetan food] and tea to Patrul Rinpoche, with the instructions to 'just give it to that old retreatant'. And for a while he regularly sent over food and tea and such things. After some time Patrul Rinpoche came and said, 'Thank you very much for all these things you have been sending.'

The Lama replied, 'Well, I am just very happy that you are doing some retreat. Who are you?'

Patrul Rinpoche answered, 'I am just an ordinary person from around here. I try to do some *Om mani peme hung* recitation.'

'That's good,' said the Lama, 'If you need some teachings, I can give you some.'

'Oh, that would be very nice. Thank you very much.'

So the Lama said, 'Yes, I have very good instructions on the Bodhicharyavatara. If you want, I can teach you that.'

'Oh, that would be fantastic,' said Patrul Rinpoche, 'because I like this text very much and I have studied it a little. Yes, please give me these teachings.'

So Patrul Rinpoche came and the Lama gave him teachings on the Bodhicharyavatara – going through it a bit quickly. Once he had finished going through the text once, he said, 'Well, I have given you the teachings. Now tell me what you have understood from this book.'

Patrul Rinpoche replied, 'I am very happy you ask that because actually I have studied this text so much on my own. I have studied it over and over and I think I now understand a little from this book. But I really want to tell you what I understand so you can say if I am correct or not.' He then proceeded to give a very detailed and thorough teaching on the whole of the Bodhicharyavatara.

So the Lama received his Bodhicharyavatara teachings. After he had received them he said, 'Well, you are actually very good in this subject. I have given you the teachings and you seem to understand them very well. Now I must say something to you: You must teach this text. As your teacher, I tell you, you must teach it! You must give these teachings to everybody who wants to receive them.'

Patrul Rinpoche agreed, 'Yes, I shall do that.' From then on he taught the Bodhicharyavatara, and in fact it was pretty much all he taught.

Around that time more and more students came to him at that place and he taught them all the Bodhicharyavatara. He would go through it from the beginning, every day a little bit, until he came to the end. Then the next day he would go back to the beginning and start teaching on it again. There was one, very great, Khenpo who said that he received the teachings around forty times because Patrul Rinpoche was only teaching that text (besides other things to individual students). But this Khenpo said that each time he heard the teachings he understood something new; he was never bored of hearing them. Later this Khenpo, Khenpo Kunzang Pelden, wrote down these teachings on the Bodhicharyavatara and this work has now been translated as 'The Nectar of Manjushri's Speech.'

In Tibet when a teacher gives instruction it is traditional to make offerings, but Patrul Rinpoche would never accept any offering. Once he gave teachings for a few weeks, and, instead of sitting on a throne, he sat on a grassy mound in the middle of a meadow. Although the people knew that he generally didn't accept offerings, at the end of the teachings some of them offered him a large bar of silver. Patrul Rinpoche just left it there in the grass, and departed - for no particular destination - as usual, with just a small bag in his hand.

A thief who knew that Patrul Rinpoche had been offered the silver followed him and, while Patrul Rinpoche was sleeping under the trees, crept up and looked in the small bag and not finding any silver there, he

A Short Biography of Patrul Rinpoche   127

started to search Patrul Rinpoche's clothes, which woke the Rinpoche up: 'What are you doing?'

The thief answered, 'I need the silver you were offered!'

Patrul Rinpoche replied, 'Oh, why didn't you say so before? I left it at the teaching place, where I was sitting. Just go and get it for yourself.'

The thief didn't really believe that, but he thought he would check so he went back and found the bar of silver still lying in the grass. This caused real faith to rise up in his heart. He rushed back to Patrul Rinpoche and when the Rinpoche asked, 'Why have you come back here?'

The thief did three prostrations and said, 'O Lama, you are unlike any other! Please allow me to become your student!'

So, that is a little about the Lama Patrul Rinpoche. His writings, too, are very special. His most famous translated work is 'Words of my Perfect Teacher' which outlines the whole of Tibetan Buddhism, primarily from the Nyingma view, but it is also of great value to all schools. He was a great and inspiring poet too and, no matter how many times you read his poems, they are still moving.

In the late 1860's, Patrul Rinpoche returned to Dzogchen Monastery and taught many important texts for some time as a leading professor at the Shedra there. He spent his final years in the region of his birthplace, many of his disciples reporting that he radiated a delicate perfume from his body. He is said to have performed many prostrations every day, right into his old age. Dzogchen Patrul Rinpoche finally entered parinirvana at the age of eighty in 1887.

[Note: The main part of this biography was taken from Ringu Tulku's teaching at the same retreat as the text of this book: Purelands 2007.]

129

130

Glossary and Notes

Editors' Note: Wherever possible the descriptions in the glossaries of the Heart Wisdom books include Ringu Tulku's own words, gathered from a variety of teaching sources. But, as this is not always possible, the glossary is offered as a help to the reader and not a definitive authority.

Avalokiteshvara (Sanskrit) or *Chenrezig* (Tibetan) is the embodiment of the compassionate aspect of the mind of the Buddhas. In Tibet he is in a male form and is revered as their patron deity. The most common forms in which he is depicted are the four-armed and the 1000-armed Chenrezig. Avalokiteshvara is translated as Kuan Yin in the Chinese tradition and as Kwannon in the Japanese, represented in female form. The mantra of Avalokiteshvara, *Om Mani Padme Hung*, is one of the most powerful of all mantras. See also *Om mani padme hung.*

Bardo (Tibetan) literally means 'in between.' It can also be translated as 'in transit' or 'transient.' Sometimes the term Bardo is reserved for the experience after death, before the next rebirth, but more widely the term can also refer to any time. Every situation and every moment and every experience is a bardo experience, because it is a transient experience. It is something transitory, between things; it does not stay put. The whole cycle of life and death can be described in terms of bardos, sometimes as the Four Bardos or the Six Bardos. The Four Bardos are the Bardo of Life, the Bardo of Death, the Bardo of Dharmata and the Bardo of Becoming.

Bodhicharyavatara (Sanskrit) also known as *The Bodhisattvacharyavatara* is an 8th century Mahayana text, outlining the path of the Bodhisattva. It was composed by Shantideva, a great scholar, at the famous Nalanda Monastery in Northern India. It found wide acclaim almost immediately in India and rapidly spread. It was translated into Tibetan during the 9th century. It is the key text for anyone following the Bodhisattvayana (Mahayana) or Vajrayana path. There are many

Glossary and Notes 131

translations into English from several languages. One is *The Bodhisattva's Way of Life* translated by the Padmakara Translation Group from Tibetan, revised edition: Shambhala 2006.

Bodhicitta (Sanskrit; *byang chub kyi sems* Tibetan) is the heart essence of the Buddha, of enlightenment. The root of the word, *Bodh*, means 'to know, to have the full understanding' and *citta* refers to the heart-mind or 'heart feeling'. In a practical sense, Bodhicitta is compassion imbued with wisdom.

Bodhisattva (Sanskrit; *changchub sempa* Tibetan) comes from the root *bodh* which means to know, to have the full understanding. The term describes a being who has made a commitment to work for the benefit of others to bring them to a state of lasting peace and happiness and freedom from all suffering. A Bodhisattva does not have to be a Buddhist but can come from any spiritual tradition or none. The key thing is that they have this compassionate wish to free all beings from suffering, informed by the wisdom of knowing this freedom is possible.

Bodhisattvayana see *Mahayana*.

Buddha Shakyamuni, the historical Buddha, was born a Prince in North East India about 500 B.C.E. and left home to discover the causes of suffering. He gave the teachings that have come down the centuries to be called Buddhism.

Buddhanature / Buddha nature (*Sugatagarba* Sanskrit; *bde gshegs snying po* Tibetan) refers to the fundamental, true nature of all beings, free from all obscurations and distortions. Ultimately, our true nature and the true nature of all beings is inseparable from the nature of Buddha. It is the 'primordial goodness' of sentient beings, an innate all-pervasive primordial purity.

Chenrezig (Tibetan) see *Avalokiteshvara*.

Chöd (Tibetan), literally meaning 'cutting through,' is a practice based on the Prajnaparamita Sutra (see below). The realised Tibetan female teacher, Machig Labdrön, set down the system of practice, after having received teachings from the Indian Mahasiddha Padampa Sangyé. The purpose of the practice is to cut through all aversion and attachment, all ego-clinging or clinging to a 'self.'

132 *Glossary and Notes*

Chögyam Trungpa Rinpoche (1939 – 1987) was a Buddhist teacher of the Kagyu lineage. He was one of the first Lamas to teach in English and was instrumental in establishing Tibetan Buddhism in the West, particularly America, where he founded the Naropa Institute, Shambala Training and the Nalanda Translation Committee. He headed numerous meditation centres in America and Europe and is the author of many books on Buddhist philosophy and practice. He was not only a meditation master and scholar but also a poet and artist.

Deity / Deities (*istadevata* Sanskrit; *yidam* Tibetan) in Buddhism, are representations of the embodiment of enlightened mind. They are visualised or depicted in various forms to bring out different aspects of its essential purity. During formal practice a deity may be visualised in front of or above the practitioner or as the practitioner him or herself. Deities encourage us to see the pure state of reality, by which we mean the state that does not bind us or create problems and is, therefore, a liberating state.

Devas (Sanskrit) are the inhabitants of the 'god realm' and also nature spirits.

Dewachen (Tibetan; *Sukhavati* Sanskrit) is the 'Pureland' of Buddha Amitabha: a state of mind of ultimate peace and happiness. It is said that if you follow the four Pureland practices, you will be born into the Pureland of Amitabha. These are: 1. Generating Bodhicitta. 2. Doing positive things as often as possible. 3. Always thinking of, or focusing on, pure qualities and seeing the pure side of things. 4. Praying to be reborn in the Pureland and focusing your mind on Buddha Amitabha.

Dharma (Sanskrit; *chö* Tibetan) The word dharma has many meanings. In its widest sense it means all that can be known, or the way things are. The other main meaning is the teachings of the Buddha; also called the Buddhadharma.

Dharmata (Sanskrit; *chonyi* Tibetan) is the ultimate nature or reality of things; synonymous with Emptiness. See *emptiness*.

Dilgo Khyentse Rinpoche (1910 - 1991) was an outstanding Dzogchen master and lineage holder of the Nyingma School of Tibetan Buddhism. He was a root teacher of Ringu Tulku.

Glossary and Notes   133

Dzogchen, also known as The Great Perfection and Ati Yoga, Dzogchen comprises the highest teachings of the Nyingma School. It is both the final and ultimate teaching, and the heart of the teachings of all the Buddhas. Though generally associated with the Nyingma School, Dzogchen has been practised throughout the centuries by masters of all the different schools.

Eight Worldly Dharmas are: gain and loss, pleasure and pain, praise and blame, fame and dishonour. They are all basically variations of attachment and aversion. 'Worldly' life is that which is driven by always trying to obtain and avoid them.

Eightfold Path or **Noble Eightfold Path** describes 'the path of noble beings' to freedom from suffering. It is the fourth of The Four Noble Truths initially taught by the Buddha. The path of practice he laid out is the cultivation and perfection of the eight related aspects: Right or 'perfect' View, Thought, Speech, Action, Livelihood, Effort, Mindfulness and Concentration.

Emptiness (*shunyata* Sanskrit; *tong pa nyi* Tibetan) The Buddha taught in the second turning of the wheel of Dharma, that all phenomena have no real, independent existence of their own. They only appear to exist as separate, nameable entities because of the way we commonly, conceptually, see things. But in themselves, all things are 'empty' of inherent existence. This includes our 'self', which we habitually unconsciously mistake to be an independently-existing, separate phenomenon. Instead, everything exists in an interdependent way and this is what the term emptiness refers to. Ringu Tulku says in *Like Dreams and Clouds*: 'Emptiness does not mean there is nothing; emptiness means the way everything is, the way everything magically manifests.'

Five Aggregates (*skandhas* Sanskrit), according to the Buddhist view, are our basic constituents. They are: form; feelings and sensations; perceptions; mental formations and concepts; and consciousness. We are no more than aggregates - 'bundles' or 'heaps' – of these, all of which come and go, arise and fall away. Yet we build a concept of a lasting, unchanging self somewhere at the core of these. This is our basic misunderstanding, which leads to our way of experiencing, and thereby to suffering.

Five wrong livelihoods for a lay person are: trading weapons; trading in human beings (such as slavery); trading in intoxicating drinks and narcotics; trading in poisons; handling animal flesh such as a butcher, or killing animals – any business in meat. The list of wrong livelihoods for a monastic is countless.

Four contemplations are based on the four limitless qualities we can develop: loving-kindness, compassion, joy and equanimity. One version of the common prayer for contemplating these is:

May all beings be happy and have the causes of happiness.

May they be free from suffering and all the causes of suffering.

May they never be separate from great joy untainted by suffering,

And may they dwell in natural peace, free from attachment and aversion.

Gampopa (1079 – 1153) was the foremost disciple of Milarepa. He was a skilled physician and family man until an epidemic took the lives of his wife and children, at which point he became a monk and dedicated his life to Dharma. He received teachings from many sources and brought together earlier streams of Kadampa and Mahamudra teaching lineages within the Kagyu school. He had many students, among them Düsum Khyenpa who became the first Karmapa. Gampopa wrote *'The Jewel Ornament of Liberation'* which is now a seminal Kagyu text.

Gelug is one of the four main schools of Tibetan Buddhism. It was founded by the great Tsongkhapa (1357-1419) in the 15th century. Based on the Kadampa tradition founded by Atisha, it spread quickly through the activity of Tsongkhapa's many illustrious disciples, and eventually became the predominant school in Tibet, with major centres around Lhasa and in Amdo. The Dalai Lamas and the Panchen Lamas follow this school. The other main schools are Kagyu, Nyingma and Sakya (see below).

Gesar of Ling is an epic narrative, believed to date from the 12th century that relates the heroic deeds of Gesar the fearless lord of the legendary kingdom of Ling. The epic exists in numerous versions, each with many variants, and is reputed to be the longest in the world.

Guru Rinpoche/Guru Padmasambhava was an 8th century Indian Buddhist Master. He was invited by King Trison Detson to re-establish Buddhism in Tibet, including dealing with the negative influences which were hindering the work of Buddhist monks under Shantarakshita. Together with Shantarakshita, he supervised the translation of the Dharma into the Tibetan language. Guru Rinpoche left Tibet in 774 C.E. without having completed the full transmission

Glossary and Notes 135

of *Dzogchen* – the path to enlightenment. Seeing that the times were not ripe, he buried further texts on Dzogchen (see *terma* below) to be unearthed and studied in later times. The Nyingma School of Tibetan Buddhism recognises him as their root guru.

Gyalpo is a very subtle evil spirit, sometimes the reincarnation of a Lama who has 'turned bad.'

Habitual tendencies (*She jay drib pa* Tibetan) Literally translated from Tibetan as 'obscurations of knowledge,' these refer to our propensity to act or react in certain ways, reinforced and influenced by past actions. They become ingrained in us again and again until they are habitual.

Hayagriva is a tantric deity, often shown with a horse's head within his flaming hair. He is the wrathful aspect of Buddha Amitabha, the Buddha of Infinite Light.

Hungry ghosts (*Preta* Sanskrit; *Yidak* Tibetan) exist in the second hell-realm. They represent insatiable craving and are portrayed as having very small mouths and thin necks but large bellies, thus they can never find satisfaction.

Interdependence describes a fundamental Buddhist philosophy or view. All phenomena are understood as existing, not as separate entities, but in a completely interdependent way. See also *Emptiness*.

Jataka Tales are stories from about the 4th century B.C.E. about the previous lives of the Buddha. The being that was to become Shakyamuni Buddha appears in these tales in many forms, both human and animal, for example, a king, an outcast, a child, a god, an elephant. In each he exhibits a particular virtue brought out by the tale.

Kagyu (Tibetan) *Ka* means 'oral' and *gyu* means 'lineage': the lineage of oral transmission and is also known as the 'Lineage of Meaning and Blessing' or the 'Practice Lineage'. It traces its origins to the primordial Buddha, Dorje Chang (Vajradhara) and the great Indian master and yogi, Tilopa. It is one of the four major schools of Tibetan Buddhism, and is headed by H.H. the Karmapa, currently H.H. XVII Karmapa Ogyen Trinley Dorje. The other three main schools are the Gelug, Nyingma, and Sakya.

Karma (Sanskrit; *lay* Tibetan) literally means 'action.' It refers to the cycle of cause and effect that is set up through our actions. Actions coloured or motivated by *klesha* (see below), for example, anger or desire, will tend to create results in keeping with that action and also increase our tendency to do similar actions. These tendencies become ingrained in us and become our habitual way of being, which is our karma. According to our level of awareness, we can change our karma through consciously refining our actions.

Karmapa is the name given to the head of the Kagyu school of Tibetan Buddhism. The lineage of reincarnations goes back to Düsum Khyenpa (1110 – 1193). They were the first *Tulkus* to be recognised in Tibet. See also *Kagyu* and *Tulku*.

Khenpo is the highest academic title in the Kagyu lineage, awarded to one who has successfully completed the ten-year study course of the Shedra, and taken their studies further. It is roughly equivalent to a Ph.D. in status. It can also be the title given to an abbot of a monastery.

Kleshas (Sanskrit; *nyön mong* Tibetan) are translated as mental defilements, mind poisons or negative emotions. They include any emotion or mind state that disturbs or distorts consciousness. They bring forth our experience of suffering and prevent our experience of love, joy and happiness. The three main kleshas are desire, anger and ignorance. Combinations of these give rise to the five kleshas, which are these three plus pride and envy / jealousy.

Kublai Khan was a 13th century Emperor of China and Mongolia. His empire stretched from the Pacific to the Black Sea, from modern Siberia to Afghanistan.

Labrang is the private household or Trust of an important Lama. All the income of the Lama goes to this labrang and all the expenditure both personal and on behalf of the Lama is met by this Trust. The labrang will attend to the appropriate ceremonies on the Lama's death and will be responsible for recognising his/her next incarnation; their enthronement, education and affairs generally. In the modern world outside Tibet, a 'labrang' is not legally recognised and a Trust is usually established to fulfil the same role.

Glossary and Notes   137

Lama (Tibetan; *guru* Sanskrit) means teacher or master. *La* refers to there being nobody higher in terms of spiritual accomplishment and *ma* refers to compassion like a mother. Thus both wisdom and compassion are brought to fruition together in the Lama.

Longchenpa (1308-1364) was one of the most brilliant teachers of the Nyingma lineage and a foremost master of Dzogchen. He is acknowledged by all schools of Tibetan Buddhism as one of Tibet's greatest teachers. His writings cover all aspects of the Buddhist path but his major work is the *Seven Treasures* which summarizes the previous 600 years of Buddhist thought in Tibet. He transmitted the Longchen Nyingtig cycle of teachings to Jigme Lingpa, which has become one of the most widely practised. He was abbot of Samye, the first Buddhist monastery in Tibet, but spent most of his life travelling or in retreat. For further information see his biography *Buddha Mind* by Tulku Thondup, Snow Lion, 1989.

Madhyamika (Sanskrit) literally means 'The Middle Way' and is the most influential of four major philosophical schools of Indian Buddhism. This Middle Way avoids falling into the extremes of either eternalism or nihilism.

Mahakala (Sanskrit) is a Dharma protector and the wrathful manifestation of Avalokiteshvara (*Chenrezig* Tibetan). He is also known as 'The Great Black One' or Bernakchen and is a chief 'Dharmapala' or wrathful protector of the Dharma.

Mahamudra (Sanskrit; *cha ja chen po* or *phyag chen* Tibetan) literally means 'Great Seal' or 'Great Symbol', referring to the way in which all phenomena are 'sealed' by their primordially perfect true nature. The term can denote the teaching, meditation practice or accomplishment of Mahamudra. The meditation consists in perceiving the mind directly rather than through rational analysis, and relies on a direct introduction to the nature of the essence of the mind. This form of meditation is traced back to Saraha (10th century), and was passed down in the Kagyu school through Marpa. The accomplishment lies in experiencing the non-duality of the phenomenal world and emptiness: perceiving how the two are not separate. This experience can also be called the union of emptiness and luminosity.

Mahayana (Sanskrit; *tek pa chen po* Tibetan) translates as 'Great Vehicle.' This is the second vehicle of Buddhism, and emphasises the teachings on Bodhicitta, compassion, and interdependence. It expands on the teachings of the Sravakayana

138 *Glossary and Notes*

(the foundational vehicle of Buddhism) and sees the purpose of enlightenment as being the liberation of *all* sentient beings from suffering, as well as oneself. This is the path of the Bodhisattva (see above) and so may also be called the Bodhisattvayana. See also *Sravakayana*.

Mandala (Sanskrit; *kyil khor* Tibetan) meaning a circle, normally having a centre and an edge, it literally refers to everything that exists within the periphery of the circle. In Buddhism, the mandala of a teacher refers to everything and everyone associated with that person. Mandala can also refer to an actual or graphic representation that symbolises all aspects of a deity and acts as a support for meditation. It can also be a symbolic representation of the entire universe, which can be visualised and offered in its purest form for the benefit of all beings.

Manjushri is one of the eight main Bodhisattvas. He is the personification of the perfection of wisdom.

Mantra (Sanskrit; *ngag* Tibetan) The word mantra is an abbreviation of two syllables *mana* and *tara*, respectively meaning 'mind' and 'protection': coming from the mind, giving protection through transformation. Mantras are Sanskrit words or syllables that express the quintessence of particular energies or of a deity. They protect the mind from distraction and serve as support for meditation. Mantras can be sung or spoken out loud, quietly recited 'just loud enough for your collar to hear' or recited silently.

Mara (Sanskrit) - 'Inner demon' or 'obstruction' – something that becomes a hurdle or a hindrance. Maras can come in the form of beings, in the form of objects, thoughts, emotions, incidents or accidents. In whatever form they come, they will obstruct you from doing positive things and will turn you away from your path. Maras can also appear in the form of seemingly very pleasant, positive things, causing such strong attachment you are again distracted from your path.

Marpa (1012-1097 C.E.), known as Marpa the Translator, was born in Tibet and was a householder, married with six sons. He made three trips to India to seek teachings from Naropa, his teacher, and brought back many tantric texts, which he translated from Sanskrit into Tibetan. These include the Six Yogas of Naropa, the Guhyasamaja and the Chakrasamvara practices. His main student was Milarepa and he founded the Kagyu lineage in Tibet.

Glossary and Notes   139

Merit accumulates as a result of good deeds or thoughts and carries over beyond this life to subsequent incarnations. Merit will offset negative actions and their resultant karma. Thus merit contributes to a person's growth towards spiritual liberation. The 'Two Accumulations' often referred to in traditional texts are of merit and wisdom.

Milarepa (1040 – 1123) has become perhaps the most famous and well-loved Tibetan poet-saint. He was the quintessential wandering yogi, famous for his spontaneous songs of realisation. After an inauspicious early career as a black magician, he is said to have attained complete enlightenment in one lifetime through the arduous trials and teachings of his guru, Marpa the Translator. Gampopa became his spiritual heir.

Mudra (Sanskrit) literally means 'seal'. A mudra is a gesture, usually made with the hands. This can be during formal practice, for example signifying making offerings. Depictions on paintings and statues commonly display various mudras to signify different purposes, e.g. Generosity mudra has the palm of the hand opened outwards in a gesture of giving. Other mudras signify teaching the Dharma or giving protection or blessing.

Namtar (Tibetan) is a biography or hagiography of a great practitioner, particularly giving details of their spiritual path and accomplishments.

'Nectar of Manjushri's Speech' A Detailed Commentary by Khenpo Kunzang Pelden on Shantideva's *The Bodhisattva's Way of Life*, translated by Padmakara Translation Group: Shambhala 2011.

Ngöndro (Tibetan) is a series of practices comprising Four Ordinary Foundations and Four Special Foundations. They were originally created for the Tibetan people by the Indian Mahasiddha, Atisha Dipankar and are treated as the gateway to all deep Vajrayana practices. The Ordinary Foundations are contemplations on precious human birth, death and impermanence, karma and samsara. The Four Special Foundations are the recitation of 100,000 refuge prayers and prostrations, 100,000 Vajrasattva mantras, 100,000 mandala offerings, and 100,000 guru yoga practices. The Ngöndro is practised by all schools of Tibetan Buddhism with slight variations. See *The Ngöndro: Foundation Practices of Mahamudra* by Ringu Tulku Rinpoche: Bodhicharya Publications 2013.

Nyingma, or Ancient, School of Tibetan Buddhism is the oldest of the four schools. It is the name given to the followers of the original translations of the teachings of the Buddha into Tibetan, which was started by Guru Rinpoche, and continued until the time of the Indian translator Smrtijñanakirti in the late tenth century. They are known as the 'Earlier Translation School'. Guru Rinpoche, the great guru who introduced Buddhism to Tibet in the eighth century, is a key figure in the Nyingma tradition.

Obscurations are anything that prevents us from seeing something; they block our direct and clear seeing. Whatever obscures and prevents us from seeing the true nature of something is an obscuration.

Om mani padme hung (Sanskrit) (pronounced *Om mani pemé hung*). Some would say this is the greatest and most powerful of all mantras: the mantra of Chenrezig, the embodiment of compassion. The literal translation is 'Jewel in the Lotus;' its meaning can be translated as 'Happiness for all beings.' The 'Jewel' (*mani*) represents compassion as a wish-fulfilling jewel, bringing anything anyone would want (ultimately lasting happiness). The 'Lotus' (*peme* or *padme*) symbolizes true wisdom, which cannot be tainted by ordinary worldly misinterpretation; just as a lotus remains immaculate even when growing in mud or dirt. Mantras are always recited in the original Sanskrit, but pronunciation may vary.

Paramita / Six Paramitas (Sanskrit) or *'perfections'* lay out the path of practice for a Bodhisattva. The Six Paramitas are: Generosity, Morality (or Ethics or Good Conduct), Patience, Diligence, Meditation and Wisdom. They start with Generosity, which is paramount for the Bodhisattva whose main motivation is compassion and unfold, one from the other. Wisdom informs the practice of all the Paramitas, transforming them from their ordinary, mundane level into a transcendental level, untainted by negative mind states and worldly concerns.

Parinirvana (Sanskrit) is completely passing beyond suffering. It can mean the final entry into nirvana or an honorific term for the passing away of a fully accomplished master.

Patrul Rinpoche (1808 - 1887) was an outstanding master of Tibetan Buddhism of the 19th century. He was a great scholar and Dzogchen master who wrote the *'Words of My Perfect Teacher',* a classic for the Nyingma school. Some of the most

Glossary and Notes   141

important Dzogchen and Mahamudra lineage teachings, still alive today, came from Patrul Rinpoche. (see *Biography*)

Prajnaparamita Sutra is the teachings on the sixth Paramita or 'perfection', wisdom. It describes the wisdom of directly realising emptiness, the non-conceptual simplicity of all phenomena. There are several versions of different lengths and many translations into English from different languages.

Pureland see *Dewachen*.

Rimé (Tibetan) is an ecumenical, or non-sectarian movement begun by Jamyang Khyentse Wangpo and Jamgön Kongtrul in Kham in the nineteenth century. It promotes the study of all forms of Tibetan Buddhism, without bias to any particular school. It is not a way of uniting different schools and lineages by emphasising their similarities, but is more of an appreciation of their differences and an acknowledgement of the importance of having this variety for the benefit of practitioners with different needs. It emphasizes the harmony of all paths, in accordance with the Buddha's original teaching.

Sakya school of Tibetan Buddhism takes its name from the Sakya Monastery, founded by Khön Könchok Gyalpo in 1073. The name Sakya literally means 'grey earth', and is a reference to the unusually pale colour of the earth at the site. Due to the widespread influence of the monastery's earliest masters, especially the so called 'Five Sakya Patriarchs', it quickly developed into one of the main schools in Tibet, developing a special reputation for scholarship. The most important teaching within the Sakya tradition is the Lamdré, or 'Path with Its Fruit', a series of meditation instructions associated with the Hevajra Tantra. The other main schools of Tibetan Buddhism are the Gelug, Kagyu and Nyingma.

Samaya (Sanskrit; *dam tshig* Tibetan) sacred pledge or vow of commitment to practice or, for example, between student and teacher. To break one's samaya or cause another's samaya to be broken is considered to be a serious negative act.

Samsara / samsaric (Sanskrit; *khor wa* Tibetan) is the state of suffering of 'cyclical existence'. It describes a state of mind that experiences gross and / or subtle pain and dissatisfaction. It arises because the mind is deluded and unclear and thus perpetually conditioned by attachment, aversion and ignorance.

Sangha consists of beings who have experience of the Dharma. It may be one person or a group of people. Buddha is the highest Sangha, because he has the highest realisation of Dharma.

Shamatha (Sanskrit; *shiné / shinay* Tibetan) is calm abiding meditation: calming and stabilising the mind to bring it to a state of peace. Sometimes also called tranquillity meditation.

Shantideva (675- 725 C.E.) A great and controversial scholar at the famous Nalanda Monastery in Northern India. He was the author of 'Bodhicharyavatara' a key Mahayana text, which describes the path of the Bodhisattva. See *'Bodhicharyavatara'* above.

Shedra is the college or philosophy school of a monastery. The curriculum varies with the lineage and monastery but usually includes five major subjects: the arts (including calligraphy), grammar, logic, medicine, and Dharma / philosophy. After completing a Shedra, some monks may continue with further scholastic training toward a Khenpo or Geshe (Gelug) degree, while others will receive training in ritual practices.

Shiné (Tibetan) see *shamatha.*

Shunyata (Sanskrit) see *emptiness.*

Sravakayana (Sanskrit), literally 'the vehicle of the hearers and listeners', is the foundational vehicle of Buddhism. It follows the common teachings of the Buddha, which are accepted by all the Buddhist vehicles. The Sravakayana covers the commonly used term Hinayana (or 'small vehicle'), in effect equivalent to Theravadin Buddhism in the modern world, as well as the Pratyekabuddhayana (or 'vehicle of the solitary realisers'). The emphasis of these paths is on personal liberation from the suffering of samsara.

Sutra/sutras (*do* Tibetan) are the teachings given by Shakyamuni Buddha, memorised by his disciples and subsequently written down. These are often contrasted with the tantras which are the Buddha's Vajrayana teachings and the shastras which are commentaries on the words of the Buddha.

Glossary and Notes   143

Tantra (Sanskrit; *gyü* Tibetan) literally means 'continuity' or continuous thread (of the pure nature of mind) that runs through everything. In Buddhism, it also refers to the meditative practices of the Vajrayana, which include mantra recitation, visualisation practices, and the texts that describe these.

Terma or 'treasure findings' are concealed teachings, which were hidden by great Bodhisattvas and then revealed or discovered at a later time by a *terton*, or 'treasure finder.' Guru Rinpoche and Yeshe Tsogyal hid many such teachings, for example, for the benefit of future disciples. Terma may be actual physical texts, sometimes found in rocks or similar natural places, or they may come as direct mind transmissions.

Terton is a 'treasure finder' or master in the Tibetan tradition who is skilled in uncovering and interpreting terma (see above).

Three Jewels refer to Buddha (as the expression of ultimate nature), Dharma (the teachings and therefore path to the freedom of realizing this ultimate nature) and Sangha (the spiritual community, which understands and can therefore support this path). These three are regarded as the perfect objects in which to seek refuge from the unsatisfactory nature of cyclical existence, or samsara.

Transmission is direct teaching of the true nature of things, which goes beyond a purely conceptual understanding. It may use a combination of conceptual and non-conceptual means to communicate. The means of transmission may be 'Mouth to ear,' by 'Sign' or 'Mind to mind.' Through direct transmission, lineages of realisation are established and maintained.

Tsa (Tibetan) are channels, which make up a 'subtle body' composed of a network of main and subsidiary pathways, in which circulate subtle energies or 'winds' and 'drops'. Cakras or energy centres are literally the 'channel wheels' situated along the central channel. This energetic body is interdependent with the physical body and good flow through this network maintains good health. When there is dis-ease or illness, these channels have become blocked or deficient, energies are not able to circulate freely and function is compromised.

Tsa-tsa (Tibetan) is a small clay shape of exact design, with sacred significance, containing rolled-up mantras and other possible components, including sometimes the ashes from a funeral pyre.

144   *Glossary and Notes*

Tsampa (Tibetan) a staple Tibetan food made from finely grinding up roast barley, commonly mixed with tea.

Tsen (Tibetan) is an evil spirit, usually red in colour, sometimes depicted riding a red horse. He is swift and very quick to strike.

Tulku is the title given to someone who has been recognized as the re-incarnation of a previous realised master or Lama.

Utpala flower rises from mud and is like the water lily or lotus, a symbol of purity and wisdom.

Vajrayana Buddhism (Sanskrit; *dorje tek pa* Tibetan) *Vajra* means 'diamond-like' or of 'indestructible capacity,' the indestructible nature of wisdom that sees through illusion. The Vajrayana is the third vehicle of Buddhism. It incorporates and accepts all the teachings of the Sravakayana and the Bodhisattvayana (or Mahayana) and then also includes teachings on the tantras and various skilful means. It elaborates on the concept of Buddhanature, using the method of taking the result as the path. It may afford the practitioner swift progress, practised in accordance with the foundations of Buddhist approach. See also *Mahayana, Sravakayana.*

Vipassana (Pali; *vipaśyanā* Sanskrit; *lhakthong* Tibetan) means 'Insight Meditation.' It is usually practised after gaining some experience of 'calm-abiding' meditation and refers to gaining insight into your true nature, seeing yourself truly and directly, which becomes the basis for transformation. See also *Shamatha* (calm-abiding meditation).

'Words of My Perfect Teacher' is a comprehensive guide to Tibetan Buddhism by Patrul Rinpoche, focussing on the Nyingma style but applicable to all schools. Translated by the Padmakara Translation Group: revised edition published by Shambhala 1999.

Yantra (Sanskrit) derives from the root *yam*, meaning to control, subdue or restrain. It is a sacred symbol or diagram, which combines mantra and symbols. For example, the sign of the Kalachakra.

Glossary and Notes 145

Yeshe Tsogyal (757–817) is the Tibetan consort of the great Indian tantric teacher Padmasambhava, also known as Guru Rinpoche, the founder-figure of the Nyingma tradition of Tibetan Buddhism. Nyingma tradition considers her equal in realization to Padmasambhava himself. Both the Nyingma and Kagyu schools of Tibetan Buddhism recognize Yeshe Tsogyal as a female Buddha.

Yidam (Tibetan; *istadevata* Sanskrit), is literally a shortened version of the meaning 'samaya of mind.' It refers to a personification or archetype of specific enlightened qualities that a practitioner takes as their inspiration, in order to develop such qualities themselves. See also *Deity*.

Notes:

1. Ringu Tulku is referring to himself and his series of short teachings called '*The Lazy Lama*' series, see Books page.

148

Acknowledgements

This book mainly came about through the concerted effort of Maggy Jones, transcribing and providing much of the editing of the text. I then took the text forward to create the book as presented here, drawing also on notes made at the time of attending the original teachings. Many thanks to Maggy and to all the proof readers who assisted us at various stages: Margaret Ford, Annie Dibble, Mariette van Lieshout, Minna Stenroos, Kate Roddick, Rachel Moffitt and David Tuffield.

Thank you to Paul O'Connor who provided the design and layout of this book and put it all together. Thank you to Ani Karma Wangmo who helped us with the Tibetan terms used in the teachings. Also to mention for our thanks: Rachel Moffitt oversees the printing and distribution of Bodhicharya books generally. And Maria Hündorf-Kaiser administrates Ringu Tulku's archive of teachings, which include the recordings that formed the basis of this book. Thank you to everyone for these invaluable contributions to this work.

Thanks also go to those at Kagyu Samye Ling Monastery and Tibetan Centre, in Eskdalemuir, Scotland, who requested and organized the retreat at which these teachings were given. And to Margaret Ford for her role in facilitating this retreat, and also all the publications work in its early years. Thank you to Kagyu Samye Ling for allowing us to reproduce a section of their thangka depicting Buddha and the maras. Thank you to Jacqui Riegel and Peter Budd for organizing and taking these photos.

Finally, we all thank Ringu Tulku himself for giving these teachings. We thank him for all the many teachings he is giving, year after year, all around the world, and for the blessing they bring to our lives.

May our work contribute to a great release from suffering and to laying the foundations of lasting peace and happiness for all.

Through the wholesome virtue of this effort

May all defilements and delusion be overcome.

So may all beings be freed from the ocean of Samsara,

And the stormy waves of birth, ageing, sickness and death.

Mary Heneghan
For Bodhicharya Publications
Oxford, March 2015

About the Author

Ringu Tulku Rinpoche is a Tibetan Buddhist Master of the Kagyu Order. He was trained in all schools of Tibetan Buddhism under many great masters including HH the 16th Gyalwang Karmapa and HH Dilgo Khyentse Rinpoche. He took his formal education at Namgyal Institute of Tibetology, Sikkim and Sampurnananda Sanskrit University, Varanasi, India. He served as Tibetan Textbook Writer and Professor of Tibetan Studies in Sikkim for 25 years.

Since 1990, he has been travelling and teaching Buddhism and meditation in Europe, America, Canada, Australia and Asia. He participates in various interfaith and 'Science and Buddhism' dialogues and is the author of several books on Buddhist topics. These include *Path to Buddhahood, Daring Steps, The Ri-me Philosophy of Jamgon Kongtrul the Great, Confusion Arises as Wisdom*, the *Lazy Lama* series and the *Heart Wisdom* series, as well as several children's books, available in Tibetan and European languages.

He founded the organisations Bodhicharya - see www.bodhicharya.org and Rigul Trust - see www.rigultrust.org.

152

For an up to date list of books by Ringu Tulku, please see the Books section at

www.bodhicharya.org

Our professional skills are given free of charge in order to produce these books, and Bodhicharya Publications is run by volunteers; so your purchase of this book goes entirely to fund further books and contribute to humanitarian and educational projects supported by Bodhicharya.

Thank you.

The Ringu Tulku Archive
THE RECORDED TEACHINGS OF RINGU TULKU RINPOCHE

www.bodhicharya.org/teachings

www.ingramcontent.com/pod-product-compliance
Ingram Content Group UK Ltd.
Pitfield, Milton Keynes, MK11 3LW, UK
UKHW051011100625
6318UKWH00051B/1179